T0305801

Promoting
Better Lifetime Planning

through

Financial Education

Promoting
Better Lifetime Planning
through
Financial Education

Editors

Naoyuki Yoshino
Asian Development Bank Institute, Japan

Flore-Anne Messy
Organisation for Economic Co-operation and Development, France

Peter J Morgan
Asian Development Bank Institute, Japan

Published by

World Scientific Publishing Co. Pte. Ltd.

5 Toh Tuck Link, Singapore 596224

USA office: 27 Warren Street, Suite 401-402, Hackensack, NJ 07601

UK office: 57 Shelton Street, Covent Garden, London WC2H 9HE

Library of Congress Cataloging-in-Publication Data
Names: Yoshino, Naoyuki, 1950–   editor. | Messy, Flore-Anne, editor. |
    Morgan, Peter J. (Economist), editor.
Title: Promoting better lifetime planning through financial education /
    edited by Naoyuki Yoshino, Flore-Anne Messy, Peter J. Morgan.
Description. New Jersey : World Scientific, [2015] | Includes bibliographical references.
Identifiers: LCCN 2015040814 | ISBN 9789814740012 (hardcover : alk. paper)
Subjects: LCSH: Financial literacy. | Finance, Personal--Study and teaching.
Classification: LCC HG179 .P7375 2015 | DDC 332.024--dc23
LC record available at http://lccn.loc.gov/2015040814

British Library Cataloguing-in-Publication Data
A catalogue record for this book is available from the British Library.

In-house Editor: Philly Lim

Typeset by Stallion Press
Email: enquiries@stallionpress.com

Printed in Singapore

Preface

The importance of financial inclusion, financial education, and financial consumer protection is now widely recognized, including by the leaders of the Group of Twenty (G20). Increasing financial inclusion, that is, affordable and appropriate access to financial services by households and small and medium-sized enterprises (SMEs), is an important aspect of the general goals of inclusive growth and financial development. However, the advantages of financial access will be reduced and risks of misuse of financial instruments will increase if the targeted households and SMEs do not have sufficient knowledge and understanding of financial products, services, and concepts to make informed financial decisions. Effective approaches to promoting financial education can therefore be instrumental in enhancing the ability of households and SMEs to make more effective use of financial products and services.

Surveys show that financial literacy levels are typically low around the world, despite the widening access to financial services and the increasing financial risks borne by households in many countries. This suggests that there will be mounting challenges for households and SMEs to invest wisely and effectively as societies age and governments shift away from defined benefit to defined contribution pension schemes. Individuals will increasingly have to make complex financial decisions to plan for their retirement and for a range of foreseen and unforeseen expenditures. All of these developments suggest that financial education should be part of a lifetime process that starts at an early age and is pursued throughout adulthood. It is also clear that individuals will increasingly need to adapt their knowledge and modify their behaviors as society changes and financial access increases. To promote the importance of financial education, this book provides the record of the High-Level Global Symposium on "Promoting Better Lifetime Planning through Financial Education", organized by the

Asian Development Bank Institute (ADBI), the Bank of Japan (BoJ), the Japan Financial Services Agency (FSA), and the Organisation for Economic Co-operation and Development (OECD), held on 22–23 January 2015 in Tokyo.

The first session highlighted the recent work of the OECD/ International Network on Financial Education (INFE). Its aim is to promote and facilitate international cooperation on financial education issues between policy makers and other stakeholders worldwide. It provides a platform to collect data on financial literacy, develop analytical and comparative reports, undertake and disseminate research, and develop policy instruments. Recent relevant OECD/INFE good practices, research, and evidence on the importance, outcomes, and impact of high-quality financial education designed to promote better lifetime planning were presented. Good practices include the development of national strategies for financial education. New Zealand and Japan provide examples of countries where such a national strategy is already well-established. On the other hand, a recent OECD report on financial literacy in Asia shows that levels are still low, while policies to support financial education vary widely across the region, and have many gaps.

Based on the work of the OECD/INFE and its expert subgroup on financial education for long-term savings and investments, the second session considered the role of financial education in supporting individuals to make retirement plans and pension choices. Examples and experiences from Australia, the Russian Federation, and the United States illustrate the variety of challenges faced by individuals and the approaches taken by national authorities to address these challenges. Many countries are seeing a trend toward increased individual responsibility for pension decisions. Key issues included the complementary aspects of financial education, provision of financial information and the use of "default options" as well as auto enrollment to encourage broader participation in pension programs, and the importance of carefully evaluating the effectiveness of financial education programs in this area.

The third session discussed target audiences for effective financial education and had a special focus on initiatives in Japan. Initiatives aimed at students, university/college students, younger employees, and the elderly were discussed. The session also included the presentation of a case study on financial education for women in Australia.

Key issues identified include:

- the need to provide adequate training for teachers,
- the need to give sufficient priority to financial education in school curricula,
- the respective roles of public and private institutions in providing financial education programs, and
- the need to avoid conflicts of interest on the part of institutions that are also selling financial products and services.

Presenters in the fourth session considered ways in which financial inclusion, financial regulation, and financial education can work together to support and empower consumers and SMEs in emerging Asian economies, with examples provided by the cases of Indonesia, Pakistan, the Philippines, Thailand, and Viet Nam. In particular, they addressed how financial education can increase the effective use of financial services by focusing on financial inclusion in rural regions in Asian countries; financial regulation of informal lenders; and financial education and inclusion for SMEs in Asia and beyond. Important issues identified include:

- lack of information which provides a significant obstacle to access to financial services by poorer households,
- the need to involve key stakeholders in developing financial education programs,
- the importance of promoting financial education programs by microfinance institutions,
- the need to tailor such programs to the requirements of different groups, including women,
- the need for transparent communication of the costs and conditions of financial products and services,
- the need to rely on a variety of media and programs to reach poorer households in rural areas, and
- the complementary role of consumer protection regulation to help build trust.

The panel discussion in the final session summarized some of the key take-home messages from the symposium, and provided a call to action for policy makers. The main messages included the increasing importance of lifetime financial planning and the need for financial education to accommodate this development, as well as the importance of involving the private sector in financial education, preferably taking into account the OECD/INFE Guidelines for Private and Not-for-Profit Stakeholders in Financial Education. It was also noted that there are several key requirements at the national level in order to maximize the benefits of financial education:

- a national strategy for financial education with well-defined objectives that can identify resources and ensure sustainability;
- financial education curricula in schools, starting at a young age;
- trained teachers of financial education;
- programs that are fully aligned with findings of behavioral economics and consumer psychology;
- internationally comparable data on financial literacy; and
- evaluation of the effectiveness of financial education programs.

We believe that the presentations and discussion of this conference provide valuable insights into ways to expand and deepen financial education to promote financial inclusion and financial development in Asia while at the same time maintaining financial stability. We hope that this record will prove useful for policy makers, financial market regulators, and academics working on these issues.

Naoyuki Yoshino
Dean
ADBI

Flore-Anne Messy
Deputy Head, Financial Affairs Division, OECD, and
Executive Secretary, OECD/INFE

Peter J. Morgan
Senior Consultant for Research
ADBI

About the Contributors

Julie Agnew is the Director of the Boehly Center for Excellence in Finance and an Associate Professor of Finance and Economics at the College of William and Mary's Mason School of Business. She is a TIAA-CREF Institute Fellow, a Research Associate for the Center for Retirement Research at Boston College, and an appointed member of the advisory board to the Pension Research Council of the Wharton School of the University of Pennsylvania. Previously, she worked as an Analyst in investment banking for Salomon Brothers and as an Equity Research Associate for Vector Securities International. Dr. Agnew earned a BA in Economics (High Honors) and a minor in Mathematics from the College of William and Mary. She received a PhD in Finance from Boston College in 2001. In 2012, she was a Senior Visiting Fellow at the University of New South Wales in Sydney, Australia.

Saeed Ahmed is the Director of Agricultural Credit and Microfinance Department at the State Bank of Pakistan (SBP). He is also the Co-Chair of the Alliance for Financial Inclusion's (AFI) Working Group on Consumer Empowerment and Market Conduct (CEMC) and chaired the AFI's Host Country Evaluations Committee. At the State Bank of Pakistan, he has provided strategic vision and leadership toward promotion of financial inclusion and long-term growth and sustainability of the microfinance sector, branchless banking, and agriculture finance through a number of policy and market development initiatives. He has recently led the formulation of a National Financial Inclusion Strategy for Pakistan, in collaboration with the World Bank and other stakeholders. Dr. Ahmed spearheaded the formulation of the medium-term Strategic Framework for Sustainable Microfinance in Pakistan (2011–2015). Prior to joining the central bank in 2005, he was Deputy Commissioner of Income Tax at the Central Board of Revenue, Government of Pakistan. Dr. Ahmed holds a

PhD in Economics from the University of Cambridge, UK, and an MSc in Economics from Warwick University, UK where he was a Chevening Scholar from Pakistan.

Adele Atkinson joined the Organisation for Economic Co-operation and Development (OECD) Financial Education and Consumer Protection Unit as a policy analyst in 2010. Her work currently focuses on the development and application of measurement tools to assess the levels of financial literacy of youth and adults, financial literacy competency frameworks, and the role of financial education in financial inclusion. She has many years of experience conducting empirical research on aspects of personal finance, education, and policy evaluation. She has a PhD in Financial Capability from the University of Bristol, UK.

David Boyle is Group Manager, Investor Education, for the Commission for Financial Capability in New Zealand. Previously, he was General Manager of the Funds Management business and their funds management distribution for ANZ Wealth and a member of its leadership team. He was responsible for the end-to-end accountability of their investment product range including KiwiSaver and managed investment funds totaling about $14 billion. He is a Councillor for Workplace Savings and chairs a subcommittee on matters related to KiwiSaver. He was recently appointed to a government steering group that will review the Financial Advisers Act in New Zealand with the Ministry of Business, Innovation and Employment.

Elsa Fornero is Full Professor of Economics at the University of Turin, Scientific Coordinator of the Center for Research on Pensions and Welfare Policies (CeRP), Vice-President of Share Eric (Survey of Health, Ageing and Retirement in Europe), Research Fellow of Netspar, and Policy Fellow of the Institute for the Study of Labor (IZA), Bonn. She is a member of the Scientific Council of the Observatoire de l'Epargne Européenne (Paris), of the Advisory Group New Pact for Europe (Brussels), and of the Research Committee of the OECD International Network on financial Education (INFE). She has acted as a pension consultant for the World Bank. She served as Minister of Labor, Social Policies and Equal Opportunities in Italy's "technocratic" government

(16 November 2011–28 April 2013) and in this capacity conceived and drafted both the pension and labor market reforms.

Kazumasa Fukuda is Managing Director of the General Insurance Association of Japan. Previously, he served as Managing Director and Board Member of the Tokio Marine and Fire Insurance (currently the Tokio Marine and Nichido Fire Insurance), which he joined in 1977, and later served as Executive Officer from 2008 to 2010. He received his bachelor's degree from Kyoto University, Japan.

Muliaman Hadad is Chairman of the Indonesia Financial Services Agency (OJK) since July 2012. Prior to his current position, he was Deputy Governor of Bank Indonesia (BI) since December 2006 and earlier held various other positions, including Head of Financial System Stability Bureau and Director of Banking Research and Regulation. His career at BI spanned 25 years. Dr. Hadad currently also serves as the Chair of the Indonesia Sharia Economic Community, is active in management of the Indonesian Economists Association, and lecturer in various universities in Jakarta, Indonesia. Dr. Hadad holds a BA in Economics from the University of Indonesia and an MPA from the John F. Kennedy School of Government, Harvard University. He earned his PhD in Business and Economics from Monash University, Melbourne, Australia, in 1996.

Kikuo Iwata is Deputy Governor of the Bank of Japan and a Member of the Central Council for Financial Services Information since March 2013. Previously, he was a professor of economics for more than 30 years at Gakushuin University and Sophia University in Tokyo. He holds bachelor's and master's degrees in economics from The University of Tokyo and completed his PhD in 1973.

Prudence Angelita A. Kasala is Head of the Financial Consumer Protection Department (FCPD) of the Bangko Sentral ng Pilipinas (BSP). She has been instrumental in the approval of the Consumer Protection Framework and the re-organization of the FCPD to deliver its expanded mandate. Prior to this, she was the Group Head of the Central Point of Contact Department for which she oversaw the off-site supervision of rural banks. She also served in the Office of the Deputy Governor for Supervision and Examination where she provided both legal and technical assistance on supervisory policy matters and capital market development, and spearheaded several initiatives on the BSP's supervisory role. She earned her master's degree in law from the University of Pennsylvania and obtained her degrees in Bachelor of Laws and BS in Management Engineering from the University of Sto. Tomas (UST) and Ateneo de Manila University, respectively. She is a professor of taxation at UST.

Nichaya Kosolwongse is senior officer at the Corporate Finance-Debt Department of the Securities and Exchange Commission of Thailand, where she is responsible for drafting regulations regarding structured notes and real estate investment trust (REIT) bonds. Presently she is a delegate to the Asian Financial Partnership Center as a visiting fellow at the Financial Services Agency, Japan (FSA). From 2011 to 2014, Ms. Kosolwongse played an important role in developing the framework for cross-border offerings of the ASEAN Collective Investment Scheme. She obtained an MSc in Finance from John Cook School of Business, Saint Louis University, US.

Miles Larbey is Senior Executive Leader with responsibility for financial education at the Australian Securities and Investments Commission (ASIC), Australia's corporate, markets, and financial services regulator. He is responsible for developing and delivering Australia's national financial literacy strategy as well as ASIC's award-winning MoneySmart website and ASIC's MoneySmart Teaching program in schools. Prior to this role, he was the first General Manager of the Investor Education Centre in Hong Kong, China, where he was responsible for establishing the center and launching its strategic plan for 2013–2016.

Sue Lewis chairs the Financial Services Consumer Panel, an independent statutory body which advises the United Kingdom Financial Conduct Authority on consumer interest in financial services regulation. She is a Trustee of StepChange debt charity and of Young Enterprise. She is also a member of the Chartered Insurance Institute Professional Standards

Board and of the Financial Services User Group, which advises the European Commission on legislation or policy initiatives which affect the users of financial services. She was a Trustee of the Personal Finance Education Group until it merged with Young Enterprise in 2014 and has international expertise in financial education, working with the OECD and other overseas clients. She has spent most of her career as a senior civil servant, advising ministers on a range of policy issues including financial services, early years, children and young people, and gender equality. She has a BSc in Mathematics and a master's degree in quantitative methods.

Flore-Anne Messy is Deputy Head of the Financial Affairs Division of the Organisation for Economic Co-operation and Development (OECD). She is in particular responsible for the OECD financial education project and is the Executive Secretary of the International Network on Financial Education (INFE) and its dedicated website, the OECD International Gateway for Financial Education. She joined the OECD in June 2000 originally to work on and develop the activities of the Secretariat for the Insurance and Private Pensions Committee (IPPC). Prior to the OECD, she worked at Deloitte Touche Tohmatsu Audit Paris, in the insurance and banking field. She graduated from the Institute of Political Studies of Paris and received her thesis in international economies from University Pantheon-Sorbonne of Paris in 1998.

Peter J. Morgan joined the Asian Development Bank Institute in December 2008. Previously he served in Hong Kong, China as Chief Asia Economist for HSBC, responsible for macroeconomic analysis and forecasting for Asia. Before that, he was Chief Japan Economist for HSBC, and earlier held similar positions at Merrill Lynch, Barclays de Zoete Wedd, and Jardine Fleming. Prior to entering the financial industry, he worked as a consultant for Meta Systems in Cambridge, Massachusetts, specializing in energy and environmental areas, including energy policy issues in Asian countries, and at International Business Information in Tokyo, specializing in financial sector consulting. His research areas are macroeconomic policy and financial sector regulation and reform. He earned his MA and PhD in economics from Yale University.

Nguyen Vinh Hung is Senior Advisor to the Executive Director, Operations Evaluation Department, International Monetary Fund. Previously, he was Deputy Director General, Department of International Cooperation, State Bank of Vietnam (SBV), and earlier served in a variety of positions at the SBV, including Deputy Director General, Anti-Money-Laundering Information Department, Deputy Director General, International Credit Projects Management Unit, and Director of SMEs Finance Project Division, International Credit Projects Management Unit. He received his BA in Economics from the Foreign Trade University, Viet Nam, a Post Graduate Diploma of Banking and Finance from Curtin University of Technology, Australia, and an MPP from Saitama University, Japan.

Takao Ochi was appointed Parliamentary Vice-Minister of the Cabinet Office in September 2014. He is in charge of financial services, administrative and regulatory reform, women's empowerment, and measures for the declining birthrate. He served as secretary to a member of the House of Representatives and Executive Secretary to the Minister of State before he was elected to the House of Representatives for the first time in September 2005. During his past terms at the House of Representatives, he served as Director of the Committee on Financial Affairs and also as a member of the Committee on Budget and the Committee on Economy, Trade and Industry. He started his career as a banker in April 1986, joining Sumitomo Bank (now Sumitomo Mitsui Banking Corporation). He obtained his BA in Economics from Keio University in March 1986 and an MBA from ESSEC Business School, France, in June 1991. He completed the Master Program at the University of Tokyo Graduate Schools for Law and Politics in March 2005.

Hiroshi Ohata is Director for Policy Planning and Research, Policy and Legal Division, Planning and Coordination Bureau, FSA. He worked in the Inspection Bureau, Supervisory Bureau of the FSA, the Securities and Exchange Surveillance Commission, and the Ministry of Finance. He has a LLB from Tohoku University and an MSc in Public Administration and Public Policy from the London School of Economics and Political Science, UK.

Ryoko Okazaki is Director, Head of Promotion of Financial Education Group, Public Relations Department, Bank of Japan, and Leader, Plaza for Financial Education, The Central Council for Financial Services Information. She joined the Bank of Japan in 1984 and has experience in market monitoring and analysis of the domestic and Asian economies. She joined the secretariat of the Central Council for Financial Services Information (CCFSI hereafter) in 2001. She has a BA in economics from the University of Tokyo and an MA in economics from the University of Chicago.

Jae Ha Park is Senior Fellow of the Korea Institute of Finance. Previously he served as Deputy Dean for Special Activities of the Asian Development Bank Institute, Vice President of the Korea Institute of Finance, and numerous public positions in the Republic of Korea, such as Senior Advisor to the Minister of Finance and Economy and Director General of the Task Force for Economic Restructuring in the Office of the President. He also served as Chairman of the Board of Directors of Shinhan Bank, the largest commercial bank in the Republic of Korea. His recent areas of interest are regional economic and financial cooperation, and financial market development in Asia. He holds a BA in economics from Seoul National University and a PhD in economics from Pennsylvania State University.

Satoshi Saito is Director, Head of Financial Services Information Division, Public Relations Department, Bank of Japan, and Chief Director, The Central Council for Financial Services Information. He joined the Bank of Japan in 1988, and has worked in the Research and Statistics Department and Operation Department. He joined the Central Council for Financial Services Information in 2014. He has a LLB from Osaka University and an MPA from Syracuse University, US.

Katsuyasu Suzuki is President of the Japan Institute of Life Insurance and has served as a member in a number of organizations, including the Central Council for Financial Services Information and the Advisory Committee of the Institute Actuaries of Japan. He joined the Ministry of Finance, Japan in 1976. In July 2003, he became Deputy Director-General of the Planning and Coordination Bureau of the FSA and Director of the Financial Research and Training Center (now Financial Research Center). He was Senior Executive Director of the Japan Housing Finance Agency from August 2008 to March 2011, and also served as Special Advisor to the Cabinet from August 2010 to August 2011. He became Professor of the Faculty of Law at Teikyo University in April 2011. He has also taught at Gakushuin University (Faculty of Law), Nagasaki University, and Shinshu University. He obtained a BA in economics from the University of Tokyo in 1976.

Rintaro Tamaki was appointed Deputy Secretary-General of the OECD on 1 August 2011. His portfolio includes the strategic direction of OECD policy on Environment, Development, Green Growth, Tax and Policy Alignment for Transition to a Low-Carbon Economy, along with representing the OECD externally on financial issues including the Financial Stability Board (FSB). Prior to joining the OECD, he was Vice-Minister of Finance for International Affairs (2009) at the Japanese Ministry of Finance and earlier held posts of Deputy Director-General (2005) and Director-General (2007), working on various budget, taxation, international finance, and development issues. He worked in the OECD Secretariat from 1978 to 1980 in the Economic Prospects Division and from 1983 to 1986 in the Fiscal Affairs Division of the Directorate for Financial, Fiscal and Enterprise Affairs (DAFFE). In 1994, he was posted to the World Bank as Alternate Executive Director for Japan and in 2002 as Finance Minister at the Embassy of Japan in Washington, DC. He graduated in 1976 with a LLB from the University of Tokyo and has held academic positions at the University of Tokyo and Kobe University.

Ganeshan Wignaraja is Advisor, Economic Research and Regional Cooperation Department, Asian Development Bank (ADB). Previously he was Director of Research of the Asian Development Bank Institute in Tokyo. In a career spanning over 25 years in international economics research, economic policy, and advisory work, he has held positions at ADB, the Commonwealth Secretariat, the OECD, Oxford University, Overseas Development Institute, the United Nations University Institute for New Technologies, and a UK consulting firm. He has worked with most major international development agencies including ADB, World Bank, International Finance Corporation, Department for International Development of the United Kingdom, International Trade Centre (UNCTAD/WTO), Commodity Futures Trading Commission, OECD, United Nations Industrial Development Organization, United Nations University World Institute for Development Economics Research (UNU-WIDER), International Labour Organization, United States Agency for International Development, and International Development Research Centre. He holds a DPhil in economics from Oxford University and a BSc in economics from the London School of Economics.

Nobuyoshi Yamori is Professor of the Research Institute for Economics and Business Administration, Kobe University. He was born in Shiga Prefecture and graduated from Shiga University in 1986. He received a master's degree from Kobe University in 1988 and a PhD from Nagoya University in 1996. Before becoming a professor at Kobe University in 2014, he taught at Himeji Dokkyo University and Nagoya University. Currently, he is also a visiting professor of Nagoya University and a member of the FSA's Financial System Council, Japan. He has won several academic awards, such as the SME Research Prize from Shoko Research Institute and Encouraging Prize from Japan Academic Society of Financial Planning.

Naoyuki Yoshino assumed the position of Dean of the Asian Development Bank Institute in April 2014. He obtained his PhD from Johns Hopkins University in 1979. He was a visiting scholar at MIT and a visiting professor at New South Wales University (Australia), Institute d'Etudes politiques de Paris (Paris), and Gothenburg University (Sweden). He was an assistant professor at the State University of New York at Buffalo before he joined Keio University in 1991. He was appointed as Chair of Financial Planning Standard Board in 2007. In 2004, he became Director and in 2014 Chief Advisor of the FSA Institute, Japan.

Anna Zelentsova heads the project consultancy group assigned by the Ministry of Finance of the Russian Federation to implement the National Financial Literacy Program running in partnership with the World Bank.

She is a member of the OECD-INFE Advisory Council. From 2012, she also represents the Russian Federation as Co-chair of the G20 Global Partnership for Financial Inclusion. Previously working as the Head of the Russian Branch of the Prince of Wales International Business Leaders Forum (2006–2009), she started cross-sectoral partnership initiatives in financial literacy in the Russian Federation. She also co-chaired the Coordination Committee on Financial Literacy under the Federal Duma and the Ministry of Finance umbrella aimed to advocate and coordinate public policy initiatives and share best practices. She holds an honors degree in teaching social studies and law, a PhD in Education, an MA in public policy and economics, and an MBA from the Moscow School of Political Studies. She was accredited in 2008 by the Overseas Development Institute and the International Business Leaders Forum as a professional broker of multi-sector Partnerships for Sustainable Development.

Abbreviations

ADBI	Asian Development Bank Institute
AFPAC	Asian Financial Partnership Center
APEC	Asia-Pacific Economic Cooperation
APRA	Australian Prudential Regulatory Authority
ASEAN	Association of Southeast Asian Nations
ASFA	Association of Superannuation Funds of Australia
ASIC	Australian Securities and Investments Commission
BoJ	Bank of Japan
BSP	Bangko Sentral ng Pilipinas
CAA	Consumer Affairs Agency
CCFSI	Central Council for Financial Services Information
CFFC	Commission for Financial Capability
CPFE	Committee for the Promotion of Financial Education
DB	defined benefit
DC	defined contribution
EFLP	Economic and Financial Learning Program
FSA	Financial Services Agency, Japan
G20	Group of Twenty
GIAJ	General Insurance Association of Japan
INFE	International Network on Financial Education
IPO	initial public offering
IPOP	IPO Pride of the Provinces
JILI	Japan Institute of Life Insurance
MBO	micro-banking office
MEXT	Ministry of Education, Culture, Sports, Science and Technology

NGO	nongovernment organization
OECD	Organisation for Economic Co-operation and Development
PISA	Programme for International Student Assessment
SEC	Securities and Exchange Commission
SET	Stock Exchange of Thailand
SMEs	small and medium-sized enterprises
UK	United Kingdom

Contents

Welcoming Remarks

Takao Ochi, Parliamentary Vice-Minister, Cabinet Office, Japan: I am Takao Ochi, Parliamentary Vice-Minister of the Cabinet Office. First, on behalf of the host country, I am pleased to welcome you all to this symposium. Besides senior officials of OECD and ADBI, this symposium is being attended by

- Chairman Muliaman D. Hadad of the Indonesian Financial Services Authority,
- Mr. Nguyen Vinh Hung, Deputy Director General of the International Cooperation Department of the State Bank of Vietnam,
- Mr. Saeed Ahmed of the State Bank of Pakistan,
- Ms. Atty. Prudence Angelita A. Kasala of Bangko Sentral ng Pilipinas,
- Ms. Anna Zelentsova of the Russian Ministry of Finance, and
- Mr. Miles Larbey of the Australian Securities and Investments Commission

as well as other distinguished participants.

The Role of Financial Services in Ending Deflation and Financial Education

Now, I would like to briefly present our current economic strategy and the role of financial education. Since the Abe administration took office in 2012, we have been carrying out the "Three Arrows" strategy of Abenomics. The three arrows comprise a "Bold Monetary Policy," "Flexible Fiscal Policy," and "Growth Strategy for Promoting Investment," and these are implemented in an integrated and intensive manner. Our utmost aim is to break free from the prolonged deflationary stagnation and to revitalize the economy.

In implementing this Abenomics strategy, the Financial Services Agency, Japan (FSA) has been pursuing three targets in the field of finance: Specifically, the first target is to revitalize the dormant household assets of more than 1,600 trillion yen and to mobilize them to support economic growth. The second target is to grow with Asia by fulfilling Asia's enormous potential. The third target is to promote entrepreneurship and to enhance corporate competitiveness.

Let me elaborate a little about the measures for the first target. We introduced the Nippon Individual Savings Account (NISA), which is an arrangement of the Individual Savings Account (ISA) in the United Kingdom and a new tax exemption program for investment by individuals in Japan. Many people have opened a NISA since its launch in 2014. Our survey shows a steady increase of accounts: 6.5 million at the end of March, 7.2 million at the end of June, and approximately 8 million people have already opened an account at the end of last year. In addition to this, we have also decided to introduce "Junior NISA" next year.

We think NISA will provide good opportunities for starting investment to those not previously familiar with investment. In starting investment, it is essential that people have a fundamental knowledge about asset management. Therefore, financial education plays an important role for all age groups from the youth to the elderly.

Growing Together with Asia

Let me also elaborate about the second target, "Growing Together with Asia." To achieve inclusive growth together with the other Asian countries, our growth strategy aims at improving the financial infrastructure of Asian markets. This includes measures to promote standardization of bond issuance procedures and to facilitate access to Japan's financial and capital markets.

The FSA has signed cooperative documents with many financial authorities around the world. The FSA will continue to push forward technical assistance projects of financial infrastructure development based on the needs of recipient Asian countries.

In addition, we invite officials from Asian financial authorities under the Visiting Fellowship program, and offer them training programs tailored to their needs based on their interests to enhance their expertise, at the Asian Financial Partnership Center (AFPAC), which we established last April.

As a member of the Asian region, Japan strives toward developing our economy and our financial and capital markets further in collaboration with Asian economies, taking into account our experience as an international financial center, lessons learned from past financial developments, and our expertise gained through participation in global discussion on financial regulatory reforms.

Closing

This symposium is titled "Promoting Better Lifetime Planning through Financial Education" and discussions will be made under this topic from a broad perspective, including the latest studies on financial education and country examples for effective financial education, by presenters and participants who are working to promote financial education globally and those with profound knowledge of financial markets in Asian countries. I very much look forward to the outcomes of this symposium.

In closing, I would like to thank all who were involved in organizing this symposium and I hope the symposium will be of some assistance in promoting financial education globally. Thank you.

Rintaro Tamaki, Deputy Secretary-General, OECD: Dear Mr. Takao Ochi, distinguished guests, ladies and gentlemen, it is a pleasure to be in my home country to open this ADBI–Japan–OECD High-Level Symposium. I would like to thank our great co-organizers the Asian Development Bank Institute, as well the Financial Services Agency of Japan and the Central Bank of Japan for their very productive cooperation and excellent support in planning this event.

I also wish to thank the Government of Japan for its support to the Organisation for Economic Co-operation and Development (OECD) in organizing this event and more generally for its continued contribution to OECD financial education activities—especially in Asia.

After very successful meetings held in 2012 in India and in 2013 in the Republic of Korea, we are here today to discuss how financial education can best improve people's lifetime planning. You will agree with me that this is potentially a vast and ambitious goal. Planning over our lifetime should actually be a key component of governments' considerations in their daily actions and strategic reforms. It has also become an essential skill for individuals, who are increasingly responsible for their future financial wellbeing in an uncertain and globalized landscape.

Financial education can usefully support such long-term planning, at least at a micro or individual level. In the—long—aftermath of the financial crisis, our societies and economies need healthy and transparent financial markets that can efficiently channel investors' and individuals' assets to support inclusive growth.

At the same time, there has been a transfer of risks and responsibility to individuals. This is particularly due to increased longevity and the ongoing shift from defined benefit (DB) pension systems to defined contribution (DC) system in many countries. This means that to plan a secure future, our citizens have to make complex financial decisions—that they are not fully prepared to make—and interact with financial institutions—that they do not always trust.

Policymakers at the highest level are addressing these ongoing trends by promoting policies to financially empower consumers. In 2010, Group of Twenty (G20) leaders approved the Principles on Innovative Financial Inclusion; followed in 2011 and 2012 by the G20 leaders' endorsement of two sets of High-Level Principles: the first one on Financial Consumer Protection prepared by a dedicated G20/OECD task force; the second on National Strategies for Financial Education developed by the OECD and its International Network on Financial Education (INFE).

This so-called trilogy recognizes the importance of three combined policy dimensions: financial inclusion, financial consumer protection, and financial education. These dimensions must be present alongside appropriate financial regulation in order for individuals to make appropriate use of the financial opportunities available to them and plan adequately and safely for their future financial wellbeing.

These dimensions can help support citizens in their decision-making process at all stages of their lengthier life.

On average across OECD countries, life expectancy has grown by 10 years in the last 30 years. And I can add that in my country citizens are lucky to have one of the longest life expectancies (over 85 years for women!). This is very good news for me and my Japanese counterparts, but it also comes with challenges.

The immediate consequences are that we will remain in retirement far longer than previous generations with increasing needs for health coverage (that is unless we retire—much—later). At the same time, considering the sluggish growth of the last decade and current pay-out pension arrangements (lump sum in Japan), we will have fewer resources to live on.

The gender aspect should not be neglected here; the situation is worse for women: they tend to live longer than men and have fewer resources accumulated during their working lives in most countries.

Planning adequately is thus essential for individuals' and households' future financial wellbeing. Yet, OECD evidence including the last Programme for International Student Assessment (PISA) financial literacy data released in 2014 shows that a large part of the adult population and youth have difficulty planning ahead (and especially for pensions).

Let me provide a few examples from OECD and recent national surveys:

☐ Evidence collected using the OECD/INFE financial literacy questionnaire shows that many people do not display long-term attitudes.

For instance, in the Czech Republic, Japan, Poland, and the United Kingdom, at least 30% of adults disagree with the statement "I set long term financial goals and strive to achieve them" (Atkinson and Messy 2012; CCFSI 2012)

☐ Difficulty in dealing with planning decisions is also evident at a young age as illustrated by the PISA financial literacy results.

These show that across the OECD countries that participated in the exercise, less than a third of students perform at the highest proficiency level on the PISA scale, the level where students start showing an ability to take into account the longer-term consequences of financial decisions.

☐   These lack of skills and negative attitudes have major direct implications. For example:

- Only 37% of US adults have tried to figure out how much they need to save for retirement, while 59% have not (FINRA 2013).
- And in Japan, 78% of adults think they cannot cover their future expenses in retirement solely from their public pension benefits, but 62% have not set aside other funds to cover these future expenses (CCFSI 2012).

Our objective over the next day and a half will be to discuss and seek solutions to address this situation. Rather than enter the rather sterile debate on whether financial education is effective or not, we will identify financial education initiatives that work best at the global and regional level, with a focus on improving individual pension management decisions. We will also consider how the combination of financial inclusion, regulation, and education can best cater to Asian challenges.

In doing so, the work of the OECD and its network of financial education experts from over 100 countries will certainly be instrumental, and I am thrilled to note that Japanese authorities are supportive and increasingly active in its substantial work.

This work includes support to the implementation of national strategies for financial education: currently over 55 countries can be considered as developing a national strategy—I acknowledge Japan's significant efforts in this area and support the government in revising its national strategy for financial education. The current INFE work will lead to a Policy Handbook on Implementing National Strategies to be delivered to the G20 this year.

The discussions today and tomorrow will also be served well by the OECD and its network, including

- the dedicated subgroup on financial education for long-term savings and investment, and in particular its first research and literature review which will be sketched out in the first session of the day;
- past and ongoing work on financial education to support retirement planning including the result of an INFE survey which will be described in session 2;

- dedicated work and guidance on target groups of the population such as youth and women;
- a forthcoming report on financial education in Asia and the Pacific notably stemming from the Asian seminar held in Thailand last December; as well as
- the newly created INFE research committee, which includes the eminent Prof. Elsa Fornero and Dr. Jabonn Kim, both here with us today.

Support in addressing these issues is also found in this room. There are over 30 countries represented here today as well as international organizations and the academic community—officials, experts, and researchers with vast expertise and know-how who are ready and willing to share their practical experiences and views.

Let me now take you quickly through the highlights of our agenda before giving you the floor: This morning, a first roundtable of experts and officials will share their experiences on efficient ways to promote financial education internationally and in the Asia and Pacific region. Next, a panel of officials and researchers will lead the discussion on the contribution of financial education to pension management. We will end the day with a lively panel on how best to address the particular needs and preferences of target audiences—and in particular youth, women, and the elderly. Tomorrow, I am looking forward to hearing the insights from the Deputy Governor of the Central Bank of Japan, Mr. Kikuo Iwata, and the panel of Asian experts which will discuss financial inclusion, regulation, and education in Asia.

This program should provide us with a sound platform to identify avenues to enhance the effectiveness and relevance of financial education in improving lifetime planning. The OECD and its network are committed to breaking new grounds on these issues with a particular focus on saving for retirement which is a concern in many countries. We are committed to the search for better, evidence-based policies.

Our discussions today and OECD work with key partners will, I believe, enable us to provide you and your colleagues around the world with practical tools and guidance to develop the right policies and programs in this area.

Thank you. I wish you a good and fruitful discussion.

Financial Education: What Can It Achieve?
Research, Good Practices, and Evidence

Jae-Ha Park, Deputy Dean, ADBI: Good morning, everybody. As Mr. Tamaki and Mr. Ochi nicely explained, we now understand clearly why this topic is very important. Many people wondered why this topic was selected through the G20 forum in 2010. But this topic is becoming more and more important in relation to fiscal sustainability, long-term planning, pension reform, etc., of many countries. So, financial education is not only important for individuals, but also for the fiscal and monetary policies of many countries.

Mr. Ochi explained how this topic is even related to Abenomics. So, this topic is really important. Also, Mr. Tamaki very nicely explained what the Organisation for Economic Co-operation and Development (OECD) has done so far relating to this topic. I did not know that the OECD had already organized similar events—one in India two years ago and one last year in Seoul. This is the third time for the OECD to present such an outcome. So, we are expecting a lot from the OECD presentation on this topic.

Overview of International Good Practices and Effective Approaches to Financial Education

Flore-Anne Messy, Deputy Head, Financial Affairs Division, OECD: Thank you very much. Good morning everyone. I would like to start by thanking our co-organizers—first the Asian Development Bank Institute (ADBI) for hosting us and, of course, the Financial Services Agency (FSA) of Japan and the Bank of Japan for being such great co-hosts. It is a real pleasure for the OECD to organize this meeting with you all again.

It is a privilege to be the first speaker on the first day of this symposium. So I believe my task is relatively important, but I do not want to take too much of your time. I would like to provide you first with a quick snapshot of the global context and explain why we believe at the OECD that financial literacy is a life skill; a life skill for this century. Then I would like to provide you with a summary of what we call the enabling framework for effective financial education, which is the national strategy for financial education that many countries are now developing, including Japan, of course.

Thirdly, and this will be the core of my presentation, I want to have a look at the barriers to financial education or to effective financial education, and I especially want to highlight approaches to financial education that have proved to be effective. I say have proved because it is either based on research, evidence, or both. Or these are practices that have been implemented in countries and have been successfully evaluated.

The fourth part I think I will leave for tomorrow, for a session where we will wrap up the day, because I do not want to conclude too soon. I would like to hear from you before concluding on this topic.

First, this is a classical way to start: why do we need financial education? Again I want to emphasize, after Mr. Tamaki's speech, that we believe that financial education should not come in silos, but that it is really a complement of financial inclusion; appropriate access to financial products, and, of course, financial consumer protection.

But first let us have a look again at why we believe empowering financial consumers is becoming a necessity in an evolving societal and financial context. Of course, the good news is more consumers now have access to financial products. But this is not only good news, because we also know that more than 2 billion people remain outside the financial system. There have been improvements and there is also room for further improvement. It also means that new consumers with little familiarity with financial products now have access to financial products. If the regulation, the financial consumer protection landscape, is not appropriate, they may find themselves in a difficult situation. This is the first issue.

In addition to that, we know that there is an increasing transfer of risk, for example, life expectancy; as highlighted by Mr. Tamaki, we live longer. We are all happy about that, but it also means we will have to support ourselves with resources that will not necessarily expand for a longer period of time. Most of the risks are now borne by individuals, because of the change in pension systems, typically the change from defined benefit to defined contribution schemes. In some countries, not only do people have to figure out how much they should contribute to their pension scheme, but they should also manage their investments, which, as you know, is a great responsibility as many people are not well informed or sophisticated about financial issues.

Innovation and technology provide us with access to financial products in a diversity of ways—increasingly through the Internet and through mobile phones in some countries. This means there is a growing coverage of financial systems, but at the same time these financial products are becoming more and more complex, especially investment products.

We could be in a good situation if financial regulation and financial consumer protection could cope with this sophistication and this complexity. But we have learned from the financial crisis and from the experience of countries that financial consumer protection is necessary, while appropriate disclosure and access to investment mechanisms that are functioning well are not sufficient by themselves. People need to be equipped with financial skills to be able to make the right choices, to make the appropriate choice for a pension for example, to invest their money appropriately for their future, for their pension, for their retirement income.

This is not always the case, partially because we see that levels of financial literacy are low everywhere, and I will come back to this later in my presentation.

Of course this situation, the complexity of the financial system, the fact that the environment is becoming riskier for individuals, the low levels of financial literacy, and the fact that financial consumer protection is sometimes inadequate mean some negative spillover effects for all stakeholders involved. For consumers, of course, who may find themselves financially and socially excluded, but also for the industry, which is quite often missing important market opportunities. Of course, ultimately, for governments that often have to cope with the fact that consumers are not sufficiently protected in their retirement or, for example, lack adequate health coverage. So, it is really important to recognize that there is a gap and this gap should be filled by empowered financial consumers. Again this means financial education, but also financial consumer protection and financial inclusion.

As mentioned by Mr. Tamaki, three sets of high-level principles have been endorsed by G20 leaders since 2010 on these three issues. I will now only focus on financial education, which is at the top here. I would like to start by defining what we mean by financial education. I know that this is familiar for many of you, so let me be brief on that.

It is really a capacity building process and potentially a long process. It involves information, but also instruction, objective advice, and a variety of means to improve the skills, confidence, and awareness of consumers and individuals, so that they can make financial decisions to improve their financial wellbeing. The goal is not only to change their behavior; the ultimate goal is really to improve their financial wellbeing in the long term.

Now let us turn to the enabling framework, what we call National Strategies for Financial Education. At the OECD, and within the International Network on Financial Education (INFE), we realized that, just after the financial crisis, countries were not only trying to develop more effective financial education programs and initiatives, but they were trying to make financial education a national policy. They were trying to make sure that initiatives, many different initiatives, were better coordinated at the national level, and were, above all, based on evidence. So we surveyed countries around the world and saw that they were developing national strategies for financial education.

We tried to figure out what were the main elements of the national strategy, based on the belief that no one size fits all in terms of the national strategy. Basically, the idea of a national strategy is to understand the context and the situation of a country, and to develop a national plan that is adapted to the stakeholders in the country, and also to the needs of the population in a particular country.

I will be very brief on that, but if you should remember only one thing it is that a national strategy is understanding what financial education means for a country. Understand who are the stakeholders that are active in the field and try to come up with common objectives among the stakeholders and an action plan with clear objectives.

Having said that, we developed the high-level principles on national strategies back in 2012. As mentioned, they were approved by G20 leaders. The following year, for the Russian G20 Presidency, we published a book with G20 Russia on the stages of national strategies in G20 economies. And since last year we have been in the process of producing a policy handbook with the goal of helping countries implement these national strategies; so they do not only have the high-level principles, which is providing a step-by-step approach on how to build a national strategy, but they also have some concrete information on what other countries have been doing each step of the way.

I just wanted to flag that the number of national strategies has been increasing tremendously in the last few years. In 2011–2012 we counted 25 countries that were either developing or implementing a national strategy. If you look at the situation in 2014, it is not only different in terms of the number of countries. I think we are now at 55 countries, but, of course, it is a moving target. So, as I speak, another country may have decided to either develop or implement a national strategy.

What is also interesting is that we have added a third category—the countries that are not only implementing a national strategy, but revising a national strategy. This means that they had one and they evaluated it and now they are proposing a revision to this national strategy. Clearly we have a lot to learn from these countries, because they may already have made mistakes, they know what is working well, and they are building on that to develop a new national strategy.

Just a few key figures on that: if we look at the G20 level, Australia, Japan, South Africa, the United Kingdom (UK), and the United States (US) are in the process of revising their first national strategy. In the policy handbook we rely a lot on the experience of these countries.

But, of course, there are other countries that are in the process of developing a national strategy.

I have to note here, and it is important, coming back to the beginning of my presentation, that most of the countries are not developing a national strategy for financial education in isolation. They are developing it as an integrated approach, as a complement to consumer protection and financial inclusion in countries where financial inclusion is a policy priority.

So this is the framework for the national strategies for financial education. As I said, I do not want to be too long, especially since we have all the material available on our website. Basically the framework consists of three pillars, and a basis that is very important; this is the first step. We do not believe that there is a unique model to develop a national strategy. Therefore, the preparatory and diagnosis phase is very important. In this phase, we propose to countries to start by collecting evidence by having a survey of the level of financial literacy, inclusion of the population to really understand what the situation is, what the gaps in knowledge are, but, above all, in behavior. Try to also gather some evaluations of existing financial education programs, where they exist, and try to map out what are the key stakeholders in order to develop and then implement the national strategy.

Then the three key pillars. One, which is really important, is to have some governance mechanisms to basically organize how the national strategy will be developed—what will be the objective and how will it be implemented. In some countries we see that different stakeholders are participating in the implementation, and in the developing phase it is another set of stakeholders. Most of the time, of course, public authorities are taking the lead, but they often want to also have the private and civil sector and the academic sector involved, in order to make sure that there is ownership of the national strategy at the national level.

The second pillar is about building a roadmap, and this mostly consists of setting objectives that are determined in time and that are realistic, that is to say, measurable in the medium and long term.

The last of the pillars is about implementation and, I would like to insist, evaluation. Evaluation is really critical and I will be repeating that not only for the national strategy but also for any initiative on financial education.

I now want to turn to the effective approaches and also the barriers to financial education. I have built this part on a diversity of sources, so, of course, I will not present each of them extensively. But I encourage you to have a look at our website if you are interested in some of these resources. They are mostly OECD policy instruments, but also research, literature research, as well as evidence of evaluations of financial education programs.

First, I want to come back to the low and uneven level of financial literacy. I do not want to go into detail here, but I just want to note that there seems to be a gap in knowledge, especially regarding the understanding of the concept of compound interest, which is not well grasped by the majority of the population in many countries (Figure 1.1). But there are many other gaps—one I want to draw attention to in particular is that quite often individuals display over-confidence in their ability in terms of financial issues and financial literacy. This is something we need to examine and be aware of because it is a challenge.

If people are not aware that their level of financial knowledge or capability or skills is low, they will not be interested in participating in workshops or any kind of activity on financial education. So this is something we will need to address when designing programs and initiatives.

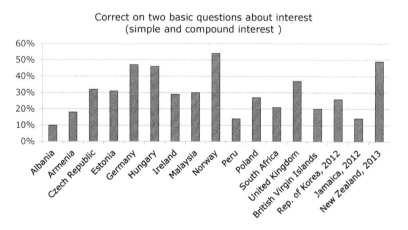

Figure 1.1   Selected international evidence: Low level of adults' financial knowledge
Source: Atkinson and Messy (2012); García et al. (2013).

Second, in terms of behavior, we know that one of the areas where individuals have difficulties is in planning ahead. Of course when it comes to planning for a lifetime the situation is even worse. People tend to be concentrated on the short term, so how we address these biases will be important. Credit is not always used responsibly in a large number of countries.

We also know there are groups that are particularly at risk. We will be dealing with this issue this afternoon, so I do not need to spend much time on it here. But just a reminder that young adults, young people, are not necessarily very good at planning, and this is an issue, because we know that in the future they are likely to bear more risk. Financial products are unlikely to become more simple, so they really need skills to be able to make their decisions. I mean, these are not only financial decisions, these are decisions for life; so this is very important. Levels of financial literacy are also particularly low among women, low-income groups, migrants, and micro-entrepreneurs.

As I will say later, we are not only concentrating on financial knowledge. Financial knowledge is only part of the picture, of course, but it is quite interesting to see that compound interest is not well understood in many countries. We know that, for example, there are some programs that combine an understanding of the concept of compound interest—I am not speaking about the math, which is important to bear in mind, but just the concept that you are paying interest on interest—with some visuals to show how it works. The result is that we see people coming out of this training having both the concept and actually tending to save more, actually tending to change their behavior. So we know that this has an impact.

I would also like to show some Programme for International Student Assessment (PISA) results (Figure 1.2). But just to show you that if we look at top performers, that is to say young people, 15-year-old students that already have an understanding of the implications of their decision for tomorrow, that kind of understanding, as well that their actions have consequences not only for them but for the society. These kinds of students are only 10% in OECD countries.

On the other hand, 15% of students at the bottom are not even able—well, are just able, basically—to distinguish between needs and wants. Typically, they are not well prepared to make financial decisions. In many countries, however, it means they already have access at least to a savings

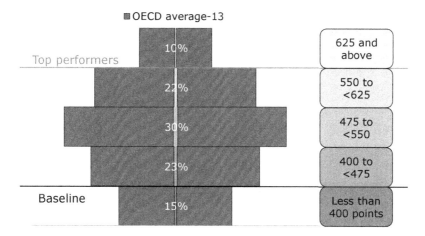

Figure 1.2   PISA financial literacy performance levels: Significant gaps in financial literacy among 15-year-old students

Source: OECD (2014).

account, but they are not prepared to make decisions, financial decisions. This is worrying.

So, what about effective approaches? I think first it is important to be aware of the barriers that financial education is facing, about the limitation of financial education. It is a good starting point to make sure that what you will be doing will be effective.

The second step, I think, is that it is really important to try and know your audience and segment it smartly. It will really depend on the circumstances of your country. You can segment it by using a socio-demographic variable, but you also may want to segment it by profile, by consumer profile— whether this type of consumer is risk averse, not at all risk averse, weak or fragile, prone to fraud. So you should be smart about how you segment the audience. You do not only want to know about the weaknesses and the behavior of your consumer, you also want to understand how they would like to learn. What are their learning preferences? This will be very important in terms of designing a program.

Of course, you may wonder how to collect this information? First, you can collect this information by using the OECD/INFE survey on financial literacy and inclusion. But more importantly, you will also collect this information through, for example, complaints that are made by consumers to ombudsmen; you can get very important qualitative information from that. You can also get this information by evaluating existing initiatives and programs. It is very important that this information is not only collected, but also reported and probably centralized in order to obtain a better understanding. Countries that did this were really able to improve the initiatives they developed.

The third step is to identify and train trusted partners. Whether you belong to the government, a private institution, the civil sector, or are an academic, you know that financial education is challenging. You know that resources are sometimes lacking, so it is really important to partner and share experience, and in order to do so well, well, you need trusted partners.

The fourth step is to develop interventions that are taking into account consumers' biases. The last of the steps is monitoring and evaluating intervention.

Wrapping Up

First, the identification of challenges; one of the first ones is the low level of financial literacy coupled with overconfidence of most consumers and also the fact that they feel financial issues are boring (Figure 1.3).

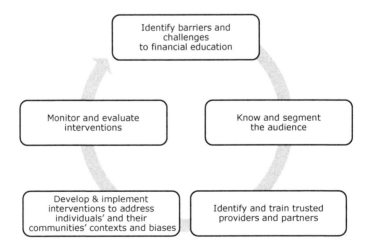

Figure 1.3   Effective approaches to financial education: A building-up cycle

Source: Author.

Second, financial education is for the long term. Most policymakers, or even providers, will want effects in the short term. How do we deal with that? Another challenge is resources and sometimes lack of expertise on financial education.

A second step is trying to know your audience. Here there is no "one-size-fits-all" for collecting evidence. I provided some examples, so I do not want to be long. There is a range of possible channels to address different audiences' preferences in terms of learning.

Trusted partners, I highlighted why it is important, but do not forget that whoever is doing financial education should be appropriately trained and that this training and financial education intervention should be monitored.

Let me provide a summary of all the effective approaches we learn when implementing financial education in different contexts. Let me highlight that trying to facilitate access to information and education is really important. Especially to deal with the fact that people are not necessarily interested in financial education, especially those that need financial education. Taking account of timing and location; people, especially once they are adult, have a limited amount of time to spend on financial education. So, it is important to use contexts that already exist, especially to reach out to people who may not necessarily be interested in financial education.

Trying to find ways to support motivation and decision-making. This can be, for example, trying to develop community initiatives whereby individuals will be stimulated not only by learning in a workshop, but by the overall community. Providing incentives to participate in the workshop but also to act upon it after that. Sometimes, especially for adults, it is really important to provide rules of thumb and a toolbox for actions, because this is really what people are after.

Last but not least, evaluate, evaluate, evaluate—as mentioned, this symposium is evaluated as well. We are very serious about evaluation, and, by the way, if you fill in the form that is in your pack I will give you a USB key with all the OECD material that I have been trying to present in my 20 minutes.

Moving forward, I think I will save that for our session tomorrow. So, thank you very much. I am looking forward to the interactive discussion.

Why Is Financial Education Needed in Asia?

Naoyuki Yoshino, Dean, ADBI: Good morning, thank you very much to the OECD, Bank of Japan, and FSA for organizing this conference together with ADBI. I would like to mainly focus on Asian perspectives. My presentation will cover the costs and benefits of financial education, the current status of Asian financial literacy and the existing gaps, and then I would like to touch upon some of the examples provided by the Japanese Teachers Survey.

The benefits of financial education come partly from better financial allocation by households, which affects not only large companies, but also small and medium-sized enterprises (SMEs), which I will touch upon later on. Enhanced financial development and sophisticated financial products can help provide very long-term financing for infrastructure investment in Asia. The aging population has often been discussed in the past.

How about the costs of financial education? It is not yet clear how much this education has affected individuals and society and what will be needed in the near future; we have to look at the outcomes of this financial education. We will also see that many teachers in schools are struggling to decide what kind of subject they should teach, and they feel they are lacking in techniques and skills. Also, at the national level and at the school level, there is a great variety of different types of education and it is difficult to figure out how to efficiently spend money to achieve efficient teaching methods.

Next is the transmission of financial education. First, it will encourage households to make more efficient asset allocation, and households will start to take a long-term perspective on life insurance and pension funds that will enhance the wellbeing of individuals. Furthermore, corporations will benefit from financial education, not only large companies, but also SMEs. They will think more about how to finance their businesses and, furthermore, it will become easier for start-up businesses to receive some funds from households or financial institutions. That will result in higher economic growth.

As for the aging population, pension funds are very important. For example, with a 401K-type pension plan, people have to think about what proportion of their money should be allocated to risky assets and safe assets and so on. Not only pension funds, but also life insurance, will be very important for self-protection after retirement. In the Asian region, financing by insurance companies and pension funds could become very important sources for infrastructure investments. Many Asian countries are relying on financing for infrastructure through the current account budget rather than pension funds or life insurance funds. If these funds could provide good financing for infrastructure, that can help to achieve long-term and sustainable growth.

In many Asian countries, there are mainly two extreme products— safe bank deposits and very risky stocks. In between, there are very few financial products, so development of a greater variety of financial products will provide better opportunities for financing investment. Then risks and returns will be very important.

Figure 1.4 shows the population aging trend of Japan. The top part is the population aged 65 and over, and you can see Japan is very lucky to have the highest longevity in the world, but the post-retirement population is growing very rapidly.

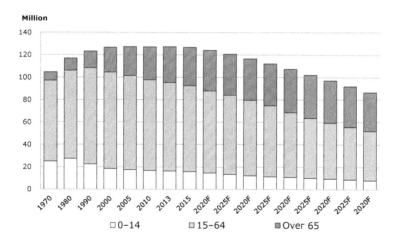

Figure 1.4   Population aging of Japan

Source: Up to 2010: Ministry of Management and Coordination Statistics Bureau National Census Data; 2013: Management and Coordination Agency Statistics Bureau (2013) "Population Estimate"; 2015 and after: National Social Welfare and Population Research Institute (2012) "Japan's Future Population Estimate" mid-range estimate.

In 2015, many Asian countries are benefiting from the so-called demographic bonus, because their young populations are very large and the number of retired people is very small. That makes it very easy to prepare for their pension systems and so on. However, if we look at Figure 1.5, many Asian countries have to prepare for the aging of their societies. This is government spending for social insurance or social welfare. Japan is at the top. Japanese social insurance and social welfare spending is very large, which is one of the reasons Japanese budget deficits have been increasing, and many other countries will develop very similarly. So that means a good government pension system, but also life insurance and self-protection mechanisms, will be very important.

Next I will touch on the company side. Not only for households, but also for corporations, especially SMEs, financial education is very important. In Japan about 10 years ago we started to create an SME database. Many SMEs have to keep their books every day and we found it became a very good education for SME owners. In the past they had never kept their books but when they started keeping track of their daily revenues and expenses, SMEs, I think, started to think about long-term

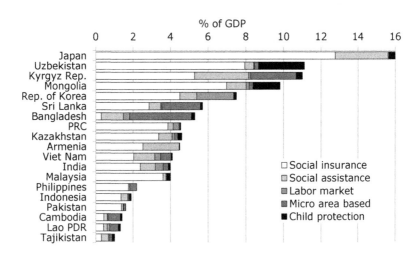

Figure 1.5   Social insurance expenditures show a broad range in terms of GDP share

Source: ADB (2008).

Box 1.1   Macroeconomic effects of financial education

• Households' Asset Allocation (Diversification)	
$Y-S = S + C = (D + B) + C$	(1)
• Aggregate Supply Curve (SME and corporation)	
$Y-Yf = a1 \, (Pe-P) + a2 \, L + a3 \, (B + v)$	(2)
• Aggregate Demand Curve (Corporate fund raising)	
$Y = b1 + b2 \, L + b3 \, (B + u) + b4 \, G$	(3)
• Increase of Expected Outputs	
$dE(Y) = -b2 \, dE(S) + b3 \, (dE(S) + du)$	(4)
• Risks	
$V(y) = b3 \, V(S+u)$	(5)

Source: Author.

planning. The accuracy of their reporting improved and default losses were reduced by these bookkeeping activities.

Box 1.1 shows the macroeconomic impact of financial education. Professor Yamori and I will discuss it in much more detail in the afternoon, but financial education will diversify households' asset allocation, which is savings. Then that will affect equation (2), the aggregate supply curve; companies have to raise money for their capital, and as per equation (3), aggregate demand, consumption and investment will be affected by financial education. In line with equation (4), that will enhance the expected growth of the economy; however, equation (5) suggests the risks of the volatility of those outputs will increase as well. So the outcome of financial education will affect financial institutions, households and companies, and aggregate supply and aggregate demand, and the expected rate of return and growth will be enhanced, but, at the same time, risks will increase.

Next I would like to look at the current status of financial literacy in the Asian region. Many surveys have been conducted about Asia and the results are very different from one survey to another. I think the OECD or other international institutions will be required to set up international surveys for many countries, and using the same kind of survey questionnaires will be important. I would like to show how diversified the results of current surveys are (Table 1.1).

Table 1.1   Selected financial literacy survey results from around the world (% correct answers)

Country/Region (Year of Survey)	Overall Ranking*	Q1: Compound Interest	Q2: Inflation	Q3: Risk Diversification	Survey Sample (No.)
High Income					
United States (2009)	60	65	64	52	1,488
Italy (2006)	48	40	60	45	3,992
Germany (2009)	74	82	78	62	1,059
Sweden (2010)	64	35	60	68	1,302
Japan (2010)	57	71	59	40	5,268
New Zealand (2009)	65	86	81	27	850
Netherlands (2010)	71	85	77	52	1,324
Upper Middle Income					
Russian Federation (2009)	33	36	51	13	1,366
Romania (2010)	34	24	43		2,048
Azerbaijan (2009)	46	46	46		1,207
Chile (2006)	25	2	26	46	13,054
Lower Middle Income					
Indonesia (2007)	56	78	61	28	3,360
India (2006)	38	59	25	31	1,496
West Bank and Gaza (2011)	58	51	64		2,022

Note: *Calculated as average of questions 1, 2, and 3.
Source: Xu and Zia (2012).

The first row is the overall ranking and there are three questions. Q1 is about compound interest rates, Q2 inflation, Q3 risk diversification, and the overall ranking can be found in the second column. As you can see here, Germany has the highest overall ranking in this survey The third one from the bottom, Indonesia, also has a very high overall ranking.

Table 1.2 shows another survey, which was conducted by MasterCard. Japan is ranked 16th, and Bangladesh 11th. I hope no one from Bangladesh

Table 1.2   MasterCard Index of Financial Literacy Report (2013)

Rank	Economy	Overall Financial Literacy Index
1	New Zealand	74
2	Singapore	72
3	Taipei,China	71
4	Australia	71
5	Hong Kong, China	71
6	Malaysia	70
7	Thailand	68
8	Philippines	68
9	Myanmar	66
10	People's Republic of China	66
11	Bangladesh	63
12	Viet Nam	63
13	Republic of Korea	62
14	Indonesia	60
15	India	59
16	Japan	57
Average for Asia and the Pacific		66

Source: MasterCard (2013).

is here, but I am surprised Japan is ranked below Bangladesh. The reason I think is because this survey was conducted by MasterCard, which is a credit card company; in Japan not so many people use credit cards. When the usage of credit cards is much, much less, the survey results will become much, much lower. Some surveys were based on certain groups of people and were not necessarily representative. That is why each survey had very different results. I think an international coordinated survey is required to compare countries with one another. Other surveys are OECD surveys, a Bank of Thailand survey, and a Japanese survey of high school teachers, which we will explain later on in the afternoon.

I would like to briefly touch upon the Japanese survey of financial education in schools in Japan. One of the problems that emerged from the Japanese survey is that many teachers are not well trained, and not

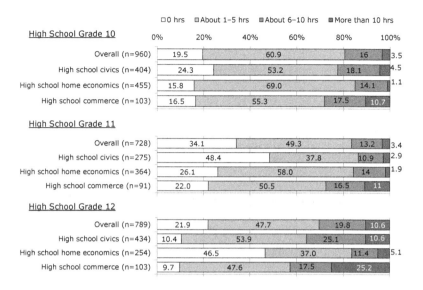

Figure 1.6   Actual lesson time/high school

Source: Study Group on the Promotion of Financial and Economic Education (2014).

so many experts in financial education are teaching those courses. Very few hours are allocated to financial education in Japanese schools. Many teachers think it is required; more than 80%–90% of the teachers say we need financial education. However, the actual allocation of time is very minimal: zero hours or between one and five hours, which is much smaller compared to other subjects (Figure 1.6).

In Japan, many students have to take entrance examinations—for junior high school, high school, and university. As financial education had never been asked about in those exams, students are not interested in learning about those subjects. I have one example: I used to teach at Keio University, and for the entrance examination one year I was assigned to create a problem. I put forward several questions about financial subjects, but all the other professors objected that those were not suitable questions to ask high school students. So many universities do not include such questions in their entrance exam and therefore pupils and students are not interested in studying financial education.

Another point is the quality of the teachers. Lack of expertise among teachers is one of the problems, and also teachers do not have opportunities to learn about financial education. I will discuss this in the afternoon session in more detail.

Lastly, I would like to talk about the situation in Asia. Asian countries have a great variety of financial education programs— Indonesia and the Philippines are relatively strong compared to other countries (Table 1.3). There are several levels of financial education— national level, school, SMEs, and so on. These tables show the different levels of financial education. The left-hand column is the national level, the second column is the central bank level, the third column is financial regulators such as the Financial Services Agency, the fourth column is private financial institutions, and so on.

In many countries various financial education programs are conducted independently from each other. In Japan we have been consolidating financial education programs and a coordinated system has been created. I think the coordination of all entities will be required and duplication should be eliminated.

The last point I would like to make regarding financial education is about consumer finance and consumer protection. Japan used to have so-called moneylenders and loan sharks. They used to charge up to 96% interest rate, but this has been gradually reduced and currently the highest interest rate they can charge is 20%. In many Asian countries, in rural regions start-up businesses and small businesses are faced with these moneylenders and they charge very high rates of interest and, furthermore, default risks are very high in those regions. So consumer education first of all is very important, and, at the same time, regulation of those moneylenders is very important as well.

Because of these new laws, defaults by households in Japan have drastically diminished in the last five years. Currently the FSA has opened up a hotline for individuals about consumer protection, and that became a very good source of information and experience for their regulations and supervision. So I think consumer protection and hotlines are very important.

Lastly, I would like to conclude my presentation. First, financial education programs are lagging in the Asian region. Many different surveys were carried out in many Asian countries and the results are very diverse. However, Asia has a very high savings rate compared to

Table 1.3   Policies and programs for financial education in Asia

Country	National Strategy	Central Bank Programs/ Strategies	Other Regulators' Programs/ Strategies	Private Bank, MFI, NGO Programs	Coverage	Channels	Consumer Protection	Curriculum
Bangladesh	None	None	None	None	None	None	BB: Guidelines on Mobile Financial Services	None
PRC	None	None	CBRC programs: - Website for public financial education - Requested financial institutions to provide clients and public with basic financial knowledge	None	None	None	Only general consumer protection rules	None
India	Financial Stability and Development Council (FSDC) launched National Strategy on Financial Education in 2012	RBI programs: - Financial literacy project to enhance financial literacy among target groups - Standardized literacy material (2013)	None	Bank literacy centers that work with MFIs	School children, senior citizens, and military personnel	Schools	RBI: - Various circulars - Grievance redress mechanism in banks - Banking ombudsman system	None

Indonesia	Financial education one pillar of Indonesia National Strategy for Financial Inclusion organized by BI and MoF	BI programs: - Financial education - "Let's go to the bank" (2008) - "My Saving" Program (2010)	OJK program: - National Financial Literacy Strategy	None	Students, children and youth, migrant workers, fishermen, communities in remote areas, factory workers	Schools, media	- National Consumer Protection Agency - Consumer Dispute Settlement Board - Credit Information Bureau	None
Philippines	None	BSP program: - Economic and Financial Learning Program to promote public awareness of economic and financial issues	None	None	N/A	None	-BSP: Consumer Affairs Group - SEC - NCC and NAPC Microfinance Consumer Protection Guidebook	None
Sri Lanka	None	Some activities	Some activities	Some activities	None	None	- Consumer Affairs Authority - Voluntary Financial Ombudsman system - Consumer Affairs Council - Credit Information Bureau of Sri Lanka	None

(Continued)

Table 1.3   *(Continued)*

Country	National Strategy	Central Bank Programs/ Strategies	Other Regulators' Programs/ Strategies	Private Bank, MFI, NGO Programs	Coverage	Channels	Consumer Protection	Curriculum
Thailand	None	BoT programs: - Financial education	Government "Debt Doctor" program	- Civil society groups and non-profit organizations financial education programs for low-income groups - BAAC teaches budgeting to rural clients	Private programs generally small-scale	None	BoT: Financial Consumer Protection Center	None

Note: BAAC = Bank of Agriculture and Agricultural Cooperatives, BB = Bangladesh Bank, BI = Bank Indonesia, BoT = Bank of Thailand, BSP = Bangko Sentral ng Pilipinas, CBRC = China Banking and Regulatory Commission, NAPC = National Anti Poverty Council, NCC = National Credit Council, OJK = Financial Supervisory Agency, PBoC = Peoples' Bank of China, RBI = Reserve Bank of India, SEC = Securities and Exchange Commission.

Source: Yoshino, Morgan, and Wignaraja (2015).

Latin America or other countries. Most of these savings are deposited into banks and they are not well allocated across various financial products. That is why Asia lags behind in terms of economic growth and start-up businesses. So, I think that the diversity of financial products and financial education at various levels—at the national level, the regulator's level, and the private sector level—needs to be consolidated.

I hope that the Asian region can develop much deeper education and financial allocation systems. Thank you very much.

New Zealand's National Strategy for Financial Capability

David Boyle, Commission for Financial Capability, New Zealand: Konnichiwa, Kia Ora, and good morning. I am delighted to be speaking to you this morning here in Tokyo, from New Zealand. I would just like to start, if I may, by making a couple of statements.

I am very passionate about financial capability and financial literacy and it is something that I know can have a dramatic impact on New Zealanders' financial wellbeing. The other topic that I am also very mindful of is the word retirement. It is a word that I do not like a lot, and I think as an industry and as a group and body, retirement does not reflect the changes that are happening both in New Zealand and globally concerning longevity, sustainability, health, and wellbeing. So they are the core characteristics that have brought me to this role.

I have only been working with the Commission for the past three months. Previously, I was in a senior management role with ANZ Wealth and I was responsible for the development, and distribution of financial services products for all ANZ customers, in particular on a topic I want to touch on today, around KiwiSaver.

Over the last three months in New Zealand, the Commission has gone through some significant changes. We have changed our name. We were, and, forgive me, it is quite a long name, the Commission for Financial Literacy and Retirement Income. But we are now just the Commission for Financial Capability, nice and simple. We have recently changed our location in Auckland and we have created a new CFFC website. So I would encourage you to have a look at our key themes, some of them of which I hope to bring to life today.

Essentially, my role is to help New Zealanders 50+, basically help them transition from paid income to what I consider to be lifestyle income. This includes preparing for their longevity while they are in different stages of their retired life. So that means that they might still be working, they may not be able to work, but we know that they are going to be living longer and need to ensure that they have got capability and financial wellbeing in place so that they enjoy that period of time. This preparation is not age driven, specifically, and I want to touch on that later.

My brief is really going to give you a bit of an update on our national strategy. It is pleasing to see that New Zealand has ticked a number of the boxes of the OECD recommendations around changes. I also want to touch on our KiwiSaver proposition in New Zealand, which is a government-led savings proposition for all New Zealanders, and I would like to finish by providing some insights and initiatives we have used that have been successful. I am here today, and the next day, to hopefully talk to many people in this room who have got some really great ideas that we can bring to life in New Zealand.

Our national strategy has a catch cry, if you like, of "everyone getting ahead financially." This term works really well in New Zealand, because no matter what you do in New Zealand, it is a saying, or a theme, that most New Zealanders can connect with. The key challenge that we have is bringing theory to reality and for people to connect to key messages, and that is our goal as part of the Commission.

We have five pillars, if you like: talk, learn, plan, debt smart, and save and invest (Figure 1.7). My role at the Commission is to bring to life what I know from an institutional perspective around the products, disclosure delivery, and sales approaches of these services, as well as the insights that I have around investment management, asset allocation, and the investment choices that are provided to New Zealanders around saving better for retirement.

There have been a number of work initiatives in place, and I just wanted to touch on one, just to highlight the difference that coming up with a strategy, a plan, and related initiatives can make.

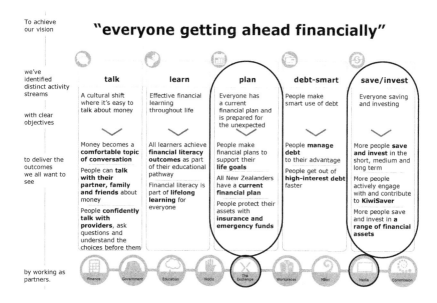

Figure 1.7   New Zealand's national strategy

Source: CFFC

We have been running Sorted workshop seminars. These essentially are 12-week programs through an employer, The Warehouse, which has around 126 branches all over New Zealand. They employ a large number of staff and are a retail distribution company. We worked collaboratively with the employer who provided the venue, an hour of the employer's time, the employees also invested an hour of their own time, and the Commission provided the resources and facilitator to run these sessions.

Before they completed the 12-week program, participants took part in a survey, answering some key questions. These are some of the main results: Confidence regarding money matters rose from 29% to 64%. The proportion of staff that had a financial plan rose from 7% to 79%. Those looking to save for their first home rose from 25% to 67%; 79% of those who attended said that they were spending less and saving more, compared with 14% at the beginning of the course; 86% of them were saving for their own future.

This is a very, very small program at the moment. The key now, and what we are developing, is a range of national facilitators to bring to life

Table 1.4   KiwiSaver will be the practical catalyst for financial education

The Structure	The Numbers
• Government initiative • Available to all Kiwis under 65 • 3% minimum contribution from wages • 3% matching contribution from Employer (generally) • Member Tax Credit NZ$521 each year • First Home Buyers Subsidy (NZ$5k) • Withdrawal for First Home Deposit • Ability to stop and start contributions • Funds are locked in until age of entitlement	• Started in July 2007 • 2.4 million New Zealanders are in KiwiSaver - November • NZ$21.4 billion FUM as at the end of March • 26 registered scheme providers as at the end of September • 35 KiwiSaver schemes • 55.5% of members are contributing • 146,944 transfers last 12 months • NZ$9,300 is the average KiwiSaver balance as at end of March

Note: FUM = funds under management.
Source: Author.

this proposition and give the program some breadth. So we have trialed it, we have surveyed it. We are going to revisit the employees after 12 months to see how sustainable that education has been. But I believe with the right information and the right facilitators, New Zealanders, and employees in particular, will be able to be in a better position to be planning and saving for their retirement.

I was involved with KiwiSaver when it first started in New Zealand and it has only been going for seven and a half years. Essentially, it is a government initiative and it is a program that is available to all New Zealanders to save on a regular basis. There are some incentives and I will not go through all the detail. But everyone gets a NZ$1,000 kickstart. If you are working, your employer will generally provide 3% of your contribution of salary and the employee has to match that (Table 1.4).

They also get a government tax credit, or what we call a member tax credit (MTC), which essentially is an annual contribution that matches the investor's dollar by 50 cents up to NZ$521 every year. There are some other subsidies and benefits. There are some really interesting statistics coming out of KiwiSaver and I think that we can learn and take a lot of that information and share it through this organization and countries that attend this conference.

A total of 2.4 million New Zealanders have joined KiwiSaver out of an eligible population of 3.8 million; this is because you have to be under the age of 65 to join. So the numbers have been pretty successful in the take-up especially given the fact it is not compulsory to join. Generally contributions are made regularly via the members' pay and this is going to teach New Zealanders the power of time compounding—saving a little over a long time makes a big difference—asset allocation, and the way that markets work. It is easy to invest in markets when they are going up; what we find is that the worst time for investors to take their money out is when markets start coming down,

We have gone through a really interesting period over the last seven years through the credit crisis, finance company failures, and now rising sharemarkets. New Zealanders have not seen the same degree of market volatility as in other countries. I expect that is because their balances of savings have genuinely been quite low. But as they grow they are going to have to deal with, and are going to need to be supported with, a great deal of investor education and information that they are practically able to use for their own purposes.

One of the other concerning aspects, and this is something that I will be raising via the media, government agencies, the regulators, and government officials, relates to the transferring between scheme providers. People are switching, for example, from one scheme provider to another, not knowing and not understanding what fund they are in and what fees they are paying and why they are doing it. In a lot of cases it is because of the convenience of having all your savings in one place rather than understanding the fund they are in that will make a difference, and it is one of our goals and objectives this year to get New Zealanders to choose the right fund first.

As I said, it is a new government initiative and it needs a lot of work to actually keep moving forward. However, the results as New Zealanders start building up, and, I guess, diversify their assets from their home—and that is where a lot of New Zealanders capital is invested in at the moment—gives them choices and diversity. That then provides them with choices when they get to the stage of retirement. I will touch on one of the things that we are working on there in my conclusions.

Investor education, financial literacy, financial capability—there is plenty of research work, practical experience, and information that has been globally available for many, many, many years. The key though is actually bringing it to life. Our strategy that I have touched on today has been a catalyst and a hub to New Zealand to try and bring to life a number of those initiatives. We have individuals in our Commission who are associated with working in schools with students, Maori or Pasifika, employers and their employees I have been brought in to deal with the 50+ age group; I am not sure if that is because I have just turned 50. But it certainly is something that we have got a very strong interest in developing and there is a wide range of New Zealanders, and a growing population, that are going to need our help and services in this area.

The education projects that we have working at the moment are currently in schools, as I have touched on, in the workplace, and in community programs, so that we are covering all, I guess, New Zealanders wherever they may be. Whether it is in the workplace or at the home, at school, or when they are getting closer to retirement and that next stage of life.

We have a Sorted website, which you may have heard about, and I am sure other Commissioners in the past have talked about it. It is a wonderful resource, but it needs to change. There needs to be another evolution of this because the web, mobility, and mobile technology need to be available in a way that all people can access it and understand it, and get really great information when they need it. But only the information that they need for themselves, which is, I think, where the challenge is. There is a lot of information out there for a lot of people. It is very hard to find that catalyst or that place to get it; and Sorted has been well designed to achieve that. But we are looking at revamping it and reviewing it and finding better ways to get it out to New Zealanders.

We are running a lot of seminars. I, personally, am a very, very strong advocate of face-to-face presentations, storytelling, and showing true, live examples, so New Zealanders can connect to the themes and theories that we all know about. So we are going to be doing a lot more work around that. We are going to be looking at how we develop that in conjunction with the media. We have a very good relationship with our media, and they are very keen to provide a lot of information to New Zealanders around this topic.

We are also responsible for reviewing the retirement income policy in New Zealand on a regular basis. That is a great chance to bring all interested parties together, and, in particular, highlight the successes and challenges that we have in New Zealand. I am also responsible for the retirement villages program, monitoring the complaints process, and understanding what educational resources are needed in this growing industry. This will be a growth area and it is one that is going to also need a lot of transparency and understanding in terms of the costs, the benefits, and, I guess, the ways that New Zealanders can work or live in retirement in different ways.

I mentioned my focus is on the 50+. Helping New Zealanders transition to paid income, that is when they retire, when they have stopped working, they have got to have the money working for them longer. In New Zealand, if you are a male you are going to live on average to 86. If you are a female you can expect to live to 88. If you are currently 65 (which I am not, I am 50 at the moment, but it does not seem that far away), you can expect to get another three years, at least, of longevity. So that means your money has got to be working harder and we are going to help New Zealanders find those tools.

We want them to fully understand their investment options in KiwiSaver and how the markets and managed funds work. They should understand that fund selection will provide the highest potential outcomes and returns, not necessarily a specific provider.

Understanding investment scams—again there is a lot of work being done on that and we have had our fair share in New Zealand as well. It is about transparency and working with the regulator, and we have had a massive change in our regulations and legislation around financial products and the Financial Advisers Act that is being reviewed; and I am on a steering committee for that at the moment.

I am going to be running a program around "What is your number?" The number that we want to get people to be thinking about is: what is the amount of income that you want today on top of what we receive via National Superannuation in New Zealand? We have an entitlement pension plan which today is around NZ$350 a week in the hand. For many New Zealanders they are going to find it hard to live long and well during that period unless they have some more money on top of that.

In New Zealand we do not currently have any annuities. We have been asked by the government to review this market. If we were just going to review annuities it would be a very short report, because we currently don't have any. So we are looking at what other income-type products and solutions are out there. I am sure many of you in the audience in other countries will have some wonderful ideas that we might be able to bring back, and I will be very, very keen to talk to you over the next two days about that.

I am also going to be highlighting to New Zealanders the three stages of retirement. What each stage could look like and find terms New Zealanders can relate to. As I mentioned earlier, we are living longer and could spend up to 30 years in retirement. During that period there will be stages of wellbeing, of health, and making sure that you have got your money working hard for you.

I would like to finish by saying, for financial education to work it needs to be delivered in a number of mediums and ways that everyone en masse can actually connect to. Financial education, literacy, and financial capability are not very exciting for the average New Zealander and can be simply quite boring, but we need to bring it to life. You need to have the passion, and the information that people can connect it to.

Behavioral change only results from regular, constant, ongoing education and information. I truly believe that. I look forward to discussing with all of you some of my thoughts and ideas and concepts over the next two days. Thank you very much.

Comments

Sue Lewis, Chair, UK Financial Services Consumer Panel: Thank you very much to the OECD, ADBI, and Bank of Japan for inviting me here to comment on some of the presentations and to share a few thoughts about the UK.

I think Flore-Anne was quite generous to describe the UK as having a second financial capability strategy. I will tell you the story of the UK's strategy because I think, I hope, there may be some lessons about some things to avoid and some things that are really important.

So, around 2008 we had a national strategy for the UK and it was based on a baseline survey, which showed which target groups were in most need. Those included young people, and older people, so the strategy was based around a number of things. First, financial education in schools. It is very important to get young people. Second, a number of programs where people came into contact with government. Maybe they needed a loan or were looking for a job, and these were touch points where they could be introduced to ideas of budgeting and so forth. Workplace schemes were also part of the strategy, because if you can reach employees, particularly if they are thinking about a pension or saving, it is quite an efficient way of reaching people.

So, all that was good. But then what happened was that the government changed. When the government changed a number of things that we took for granted, the advances that we had made, disappeared. As well as the things I just mentioned we had a very good asset-building program called the Child Trust Fund. So every baby that was born received a sum of money, about £500, and this was put into an account for them and grew, and so when they reached the age of 18 they had a sum of money that was theirs. They could not touch the money until then, but they could see it and they could see it growing. This was also a very useful financial education opportunity. Again, universal, because every child had one of these child trust funds, so it was a really good opportunity.

A new government did away with the Child Trust Fund. It did away with a lot of other programs, too. So, my number one lesson in strategies is, you need sustainable leadership. Somebody has to be there making this happen when politicians come and go—financial education needs a solid, sustainable base.

One of the gaps in the strategy was this idea that people need to talk to someone. A number of the speakers have mentioned the need for people to become really engaged with financial issues and sometimes that just means picking up a phone; it means talking to someone.

So the government set up the Money Advice Service, and really that was its job, to respond to people's needs to know about everyday money, and also to give them some education, information that would help them manage their own money better.

I do not want to be negative about the Money Advice Service, because I think it has done some very good things, but it has not really had the chance to grow and to find its feet because it keeps getting reviewed. Politicians keep saying: what is this thing about? Why is it here? Why is it spending money on advertising? So there is a continual process, driven by the industry of saying: what is this for?

Another review is about to come out and the Money Advice Service, will, I am sure, change again and grow and move forward again. So the lesson is about leadership, I think, and making sure that the whole thing is sustainable.

So, where are we now? Well in the UK market we have very low levels of savings. We have very low levels of trust in the industry. People's asset allocation is very much driven toward property, similar to New Zealand, the main asset is often the house. We have very high levels of over-indebtedness. We have had some interesting things happening with our pensions recently. We have something that looks very much like KiwiSaver, so people who are automatically enrolled into a pension, they do start saving. But the problem is they need financial education to go with that, otherwise they just do not know if it is enough money. They do not know what their number is, for example. So they do not know whether that will give them enough. They do not really think about it because it is done for them.

Now when people retire, at the other end, we have done the opposite to New Zealand. We have said to people, you do not need to buy an annuity anymore. It used to be compulsory, well virtually compulsory, but it no longer is. So we now have a generation of people getting toward retirement age and suddenly they are faced with choices they never had to face before.

So a lot of new products are coming onto the market; some of them are very risky. People do not understand investment, because they never really had to understand investment; they had so much done for them. So what the government has done is it has introduced this thing called the Guidance Guarantee. Now everybody coming up to retirement will be able to have a conversation about their options. Those options may be to buy an annuity or another income product. They may be to just work longer. They may be to release some money from their house;

and we do not know how this is going to work yet. These new pension freedoms are very, very new in the UK.

I was very interested in the New Zealand question about disclosure, better disclosure. I think there are a couple of issues here. It is no good giving people information if they do not understand it. So we know that better disclosure about costs has to go hand-in-hand with financial education. That is a given. But the other thing, finally, to end on, is my panel has done some work recently on investment costs. What we have discovered is that the money that is taken out of people's investment through costs and charges can actually be three or four times as much as the "headline" annual management charge.

So we are pressing very strongly now in the UK for not only full disclosure of costs, so that people know how much they are going to have taken out of their investment pot, but we are also pressing to reduce those costs. Because it is no use people understanding that compounding will give them a bigger amount of money if, in fact, a lot of that money is being taken out in costs and charges. So, this is another example of where, I think, financial awareness and education can go hand-in-hand with consumer protection. So you need always to think about when is protection or regulation the best tool, and when is education the best tool, and how can those two things fit together?

So I am optimistic now that we are moving forward to a new era again in the UK. We are finding ways of linking financial education with debt management, which is really quite important to us at the moment.

I think I am pretty much there, actually. So we are developing our new strategy. We will not only learn from ourselves but also from you and those many other countries that have developed strategies in the meantime. So, thank you, again, for inviting me. Thank you.

Dr. Jae Ha Park: Thank you, Ms. Lewis. I think her comments are not directly on the presentations of others, but rather on the UK's case of financial education. But, before opening the floor, if you want to comment on the discussion, actually I would like to invite you first. So Flore-Anne.

Ms. Flore-Anne Messy: Yes, thank you. I appreciate the opportunity, actually. I wanted to react on two points, first about the second presentation, after me, flagging the importance of cross-comparable evidence. In fact, the OECD cannot agree more and actually we have two tools to develop cross-comparable evidence. The first one is the PISA financial literacy assessment that was conducted for the first time in 2012, with results in 2014. We will have a second exercise in 2015, so this year with results in 2017 for another group of countries. We are planning a third exercise in 2018, and we are hoping to get in even more countries for this exercise. We hope that Japan will also participate in this third exercise. So this is for 15-year-old students. I have to say that this exercise for students is very comprehensive.

It is not only providing the level of financial competency of young people, but it is also providing a framework to understand what financial literacy capability means for 15-year-olds. So, I encourage you not only to look at the ranking, but to look at the analysis and also what we are trying to develop, which is a framework of financial literacy for 15-year-olds. So now for adults, we developed, back in 2010 actually, a questionnaire that is not only focusing on financial knowledge but also on financial attitude and financial behavior. So it is trying really to combine the three components. It was tested across 14 countries in 2012, and we have the results. Now we are planning a second exercise this year. So we have revised this first tool to try also to include some aspects that were not necessarily covered in the first survey related to retirement. For example, related to fraud, related also to financial wellbeing. So we tried to include some indicators of financial wellbeing.

So, I think we have around 30 countries that will participate in this second exercise. I have to say that this tool has also been supported and welcomed by G20 leaders, so this really is an international tool that, by the way, all institutions are welcome to use. I mean they are available on our website, I am speaking about the adult tool, and if your country is not participating in the cross-comparable survey this year, the tool is still available for you to use. The sample size is regular, so we do not only have the questions, we also have a methodology that we recommend countries use so that the evidence is indeed cross-comparable. That is a first thing.

Second, I just wanted to react to Sue's comment, which I think was extremely valuable, on sustainability. This is really one of the key challenges I would like to say. When we started the work on financial education at the OECD in 2002, we were not taken very seriously. Now we are taken very seriously, which is a good thing. But financial education is a victim of its own success, meaning first that we have come from too few initiatives to sometimes too many, not necessarily based on evidence. So we are trying to promote the evidence.

Third, there is clearly a momentum after the financial crisis for financial education. How long it will last is the question. We know that financial education is a process. We are here to build financial skills for future generations. We need to start early. We need to start in schools, but, we know, that political changes may imply, like in the UK, that financial education is no longer a priority, that financial education suddenly disappears from school programs. So what do we do about it? We are trying to look at different ways countries are trying to address the issue, and certainly trying to make sure that there is some kind of leadership and institution or a group of institutions with some independence from political power that really have a mandate to provide financial education, like, for example, a central bank has a mandate to conduct monetary policy.

For financial education we are looking for a similar body with some independence to try and do that in countries. So, of course, different countries will have different types of institutions that can be in charge. In some countries a new body is created to take care of financial capability, as is the case in New Zealand; typically there is a commission that deals with retirement and financial education, and more and more financial education. So this is an interesting model.

We are looking at Brazil, for example, where different financial regulators are getting together to build a new entity to develop and implement a national strategy. But, typically, it is important that there is a mandate and resources and probably that it is in the school curriculum. We know that it does not mean that it will last forever, but at least if it is there, it is actually a symptom of possible sustainability. I would say sustainability also depends on key partners and trusted partners out there. We know that in many countries associations of banks, insurance, and investment funds have been key players in this area.

So, yes, I just wanted to react on these two things. But I am happy to take any questions later, of course.

Dr. Jae Ha Park: So, Dean Yoshino, yes.

Dean Naoyuki Yoshino: Thank you. I have one comment about recent developments in the world. The World Economic Forum in Davos is discussing income disparities that are widening in many countries. How much can financial education mitigate those income disparities and prepare people for retirement and enhance their long-term perspectives? I would like to ask other panelists if they believe financial education can help to stop the widening of income disparities.

Dr. Jae Ha Park: Yes, Mr. Boyle, do you have a comment to respond to that?

Mr. David Boyle: So the one thing I was interested in is, in New Zealand we have real problems with New Zealanders getting access to financial advice. The advice market, advisors, and financial planners are probably not that well regarded given a range of different outcomes and I suspect that is the case across the board internationally. The comment that was made about the UK is quite relevant. I think our challenge is to find ways that investors or savers can actually access good quality information that they can connect with, not just through the product but also through other mediums.

Then when they get to a certain level of size or balance—which is what we will be facing and we are preparing for—as balances grow, they have got a means and perhaps a plan or strategy that would allow them to diversify that asset or create some level of income, not just an annuity-type product, but also have access to advice. So, I think it is good if people can get advice, but it has got to be something that they can universally use and take away and apply to their day-to-day life. So I am interested to see how the proposition of offering advice goes in the UK. The service is only as good as the delivery would be my view.

Dr. Jae Ha Park: Thank you very much, and we have around another 10 minutes more, so I would like to open the floor and collect a couple of questions. So, please identify yourselves first and you may ask a specific or general question to any expert on the podium or make a comment. So, could you raise your hand and ask questions? Yes, please, the gentleman there.

Open Floor Discussion

Audience member: Mr. David Boyle, I have one question. Please tell us the difference between financial literacy and financial capability in New Zealand.

Mr. David Boyle: So, I think the question was the difference between financial literacy and financial capability, is that right, in the sense of how we look at it in New Zealand?

Financial literacy is more of an educational process achieved through the schools, and trying to get that developed and into the curriculum on a national basis is the challenge. It is a very hard thing to do and I presume, and bear with me, my knowledge around what other countries have in this area is very limited. But it is something that we are working on. But we felt that in New Zealand, it should be about people being capable and in a position where they can understand, use, and have knowledge or information that is provided, whether it is through a financial product or service, and they can see the value that it brings to their investment or their wellbeing.

So it is more practical knowledge–just like being a capable plumber or a capable builder. It is things that they can relate to. In other words, we want to bring to life in New Zealand that you can actually be financially capable but do not have to know everything. But you need to understand the concepts and apply them to your own personal circumstances, and that is what we are trying to do.

Dr. Jae Ha Park: Next question? If you do not have any, I would like to ask another question to Flore-Anne, actually. Of course every country is different in terms of their cultures, but, for example, as Dean Yoshino mentioned, his experience in Keio University was instructive. It is true. So, in Asia for example, if the subject is not included as an entrance exam, nobody studies it. There is no incentive. Of course they know it is quite an important issue, however, they do not have to take a test when they take the entrance exam. So the youth of today just forget about it; they do not study it. This means it is now not only a matter of the teachers, but also a matter of the motivation of the students—why should I study?

So, have you had in other countries the issue of how to improve students' knowledge of financial subjects?

Ms. Flore-Anne Messy: Well, yes it is a very good question. Actually, when we started the work within the network we decided also to focus on schools and in fact Sue Lewis was our leader of that subgroup within the INFE. So we discussed all of these issues. First, what should be the content of financial literacy or capability whatever you like to call it, in the school, and second, how do we make it work? Making it work is making it interesting and engaging and providing some motivation.

So we developed some guidelines on financial education in schools and one of the recommendations is that, indeed, financial literacy, if it is introduced in the school curriculum, should also be part of the final examination. So that is one instance. Having said that, it is not always possible because the curricula are crowded, etc. So quite often financial education is not introduced as a new topic in most countries, but as a cross-curricular topic. So we recommended at least part of this is part of the final exam.

In addition to that, there are other ways to motivate students and we see that something that is important is trying not to turn financial education into a lecture, but making it practical. Because what we are trying to achieve is really to try to develop and nurture new habits, like planning ahead for example. So trying to use games, use practical scenarios that may happen in a student's life.

Secondly, we are trying to engage countries and schools to develop competitions. This is working quite well in engaging students. So this is not necessarily a regular part of the curriculum, but rather a special project. For example, how do you finance a holiday for the school, or things like that? Students can write essays or develop a plan for it. So, other ways to incentivize, not only the children but also, I would say, the teacher. Because the teachers also need motivation. So having it as part of the examination is probably the best way, using it as a stick, but you can also develop some smart carrots so that people become really interested in the topic.

Games around financial education are increasingly being developed. So I think countries need to be creative in coming up with the pedagogical tools to use. Do not be shy and try and use Apps and mobile phones and thing like that. These are the things that young people now are interested in. So these are ways through which financial education can be not only engaging and motivating, but can also be a part of students' lives. I think it is important to bear that in mind.

Two things about that. One is to really train teachers. Train teachers not only in the topic. Bear in mind that we are speaking not only about finance, which is already quite difficult to talk about in school, but we are talking about decisions in life, important decisions, and values. In order for teachers to feel confident discussing this issue in class they should really consider this and really have of course the financial background and knowledge, but also understand that any financial decision is relative to households. So there is no judgment here, and this will be very important.

Last but not least, parents. Parents should be involved in the process. So countries that are successful in introducing financial education in schools have tried also to develop workshops and seminars for parents, so that also they understand why it is important for their children and what they can do themselves about their own finance, personal finance. So, yes, those would be my answers.

Dr. Jae Ha Park: Ms. Lewis, do you have something to add?

Ms. Sue Lewis: Well, I thought I did and then Flore-Anne said some more. But just to say we have recently made this a compulsory subject in the UK. It is split between mathematics, which of course will be the part that is tested and examined, and citizenship, which reflects those softer judgmental aspects of financial education. But it is compulsory for children aged 11 and up.

Just really to emphasize the point Flore-Anne made about training the teachers, because the teachers are not confident with money either and many of them are almost learning with the children. So the resources we have put in in the UK have been very much about supporting teachers. Providing good, fun resources, but really supporting teachers not only with training, but also a help line and other ways for teachers to feel confident about teaching financial education. They want to teach it, but they are scared.

Dr. Jae Ha Park: One last question.

Prudence Kasala, Head of the Financial Consumer Protection Department, Bangko Sentral ng Pilipinas: I am Prudence Kasala from the Philippines. First of all, I would like to congratulate the whole panel for presenting a very comprehensive and interesting discussion on the subject matter.

I do have a question regarding the comments of Sue and Flore-Anne on the sustainability of the programs. For it to be sustainable, I think we have to make the case for financial education, which means that you have to have an effective monitoring and impact evaluation. The problem with a lot of these monitoring and impact evaluation tools is they take a bit of a time. So for us, especially in government, where we have to spend substantial resources, we are now being confronted with the question: is it making any difference?

So we want to find out whether there are substantial developments in terms of program monitoring or impact evaluation, so that we too could show to our own governments that this is really making a difference. Thank you.

Dr. Jae Ha Park: Thank you. Could you respond very briefly because we are about to finish?

Ms. Flore-Anne Messy: Thank you, Prudence, for the question. Yes, it is very important we always insist on impact evaluation and monitoring of programs. So, currently we are developing a database of programs that are being evaluated worldwide. We have developed a template and we are inviting countries, providers of financial education that have not only developed programs but consistently evaluated them to provide us with the information and we will make all that available on the website.

We are also developing a checklist on how to monitor and evaluate programs. So if you are interested in the topic, please reach out to us. By us I mean Dr. Atkinson and I. Thank you.

Ms. Sue Lewis: I just think we have to remember that a lot of the impacts are going to be very long-term. There is the mismatch, of course, between politicians who want results now and actually the young people who will go on and become healthier over a long period of time. They will have wellbeing, better mental health, and all those things are really (a) hard to monetize, but (b) they take place over a very long time.

So, though it is incredibly important I think we just have to make that argument as well. Thank you.

Dr. Jae Ha Park: If any other panelists have something to add, then you are welcome. Otherwise, we are already overdue. So, I think this topic is very important and Session 1 is really a good start with the overview by the OECD, the overview on the Asian situation by the ADBI Dean, the specific case of the national strategy of New Zealand, and the similar case of the UK.

So I think with that we can start a real fruitful discussion in the afternoon and tomorrow morning. With that I would like to adjourn this session. Why do you not join me in thanking all the panelists for their excellent presentations and discussion?

Financial Education for Effective Pension Management: Challenges and Solutions

Elsa Fornero, Professor, University of Turin and Center for Research on Pensions and Welfare Policies: Thank you very much and good afternoon and first of all let me say it is a pleasure to be here today. It is my second time in Tokyo and I have lovely memories of my first visit to this country. I just arrived from Turin, Italy, on a plane that was full of Japanese people coming back from their, I hope, exciting Italian holidays. We are here today to talk about the relationship between financial literacy and pension reforms. It is a very important subject and I just want to make a few introductory remarks.

Everywhere in the rich countries, the welfare state is in crisis. No one disputes that. Disputes start when we look at the nature of the crisis. For some, it is an irreversible crisis that will sooner or later replace the welfare system that we know with a system of private insurance schemes. Others, and I include myself among them, take a very different view. The welfare crisis it not an identity crisis, but it is rather an adaptation crisis. The socio-demographic structure has changed and will continue to change and the welfare state is struggling to adapt.

The pension system is at the core of the welfare system and so it is no wonder that it finds itself also at the core of this transformation. Like many problems in our societies, this one too has been created by its very success. The dramatic progress in health, living conditions, and life expectancy, coupled with a fall in the birth rate, has started a demographic transition leading to inverted age pyramids. This transformation shows clear inconsistencies in the pension design. Pension debts could no longer be happily loaded onto the young and yet unborn generations, since these generations were rapidly becoming less numerous, just when the numbers of present and projected pensioners were steadily climbing.

A political response was needed and it started almost everywhere in terms of pension reforms. These reforms have produced results, but have also created a lot of discontent and a lot of resistance among people. It is my opinion that part of this resistance and struggling is due to lack of knowledge, lack of understanding, and that is why I believe that the challenge of not only saving but reinforcing our welfare system requires a new paradigm. This paradigm is made of three pillars.

The first one is "continue reform." The reform process has not ended and must be completed. Adequate old age provision requires individuals to be safeguarded against market failures affecting their active lifecycles: lack of education, unemployment, sickness, and invalidity, but also divorce and family disruption. After years of recession and longer relative decline in countries like Italy, the main challenge to the pension system is, in my opinion, the present structure of the labor market. Dynamic and inclusive labor markets are the best premise for adequate pension systems. Pension and labor market reforms have to be better integrated and policies to promote long-term employment such as apprenticeships and lifelong learning must be given more importance and more resources.

The second pillar is "inform people." The accumulation of pension wealth is a long and complex behavior. Workers must have an idea as precise as possible where they stand on pension wealth and retirement options so that they can make clear, rational retirement choices. This knowledge is essential for individual planning and should help avoid mistakes or big disappointments such as shortfalls of actual versus expected pension benefits and ensuing painful adjustment. But to know, to be informed, is not enough. So here is where understanding and financial literacy come in.

So the third pillar is "educate people." Educate people because understanding the basic elements of pension reform still requires not only good information, but also financial literacy. Research has shown that the vast majority of workers can be described as financially illiterate. Knowledge about compound interest, for example, is crucial to understanding how pension wealth accumulation works. It should be generally realized that each euro or each yen paid into a retirement account will add to the retirement income and the longer the period, the higher the accumulated wealth, and so on, and so on.

So I think that the real challenge ahead of the aging society, to reinforce the pension system, is to make within a well-designed system people more knowledgeable and more directly responsible through their work, savings, and retirement choices for the accumulation of their pension wealth. It is an inalienable expansion of citizenship that cannot be further delayed.

To discuss this very important topic and to discuss how having financially literate people, citizens, can make a more complete democracy and help the reform process, we have here different panelists coming from different countries and they will talk about the experience of their countries and we will have the opportunity to compare different experiences and to compare with the Japanese experience.

Let me introduce them. They are Dr. Adele Atkinson, Policy Analyst at the Financial Affairs Division of the OECD; then Ms. Anna Zelentsova, Head of Financial Literacy at the Ministry of Finance in the Russian Federation and Co-Chair of Financial Literacy subgroup of the Global Partnership for Financial Inclusion (GPFI); then Dr. Julie Agnew, Director of the Boehly Center for Excellence in Finance, Mason School of Business, US; and Mr. Miles Larbey, Head of Financial Education at the Australian Securities and Investments Commission.

Findings from the OECD Survey on Financial Education for Retirement Saving

Adele Atkinson, Policy Analyst, Financial Affairs Division, OECD: Hello everybody. One of the real benefits of coming to one of these types of symposiums is that you get to hear findings before they have been made public. What I am going to share with you today is work in progress from the OECD International Network on Financial Education and in particular from their expert subgroup on financial education for long-term savings and investments. This subgroup has been working very hard to try to identify current good practices and evaluation evidence, and to try to understand what is actually happening in countries. One of the things we have already heard today is there is a lot happening in countries, but there is also an awful lot of change going on within countries. Some of that is within policymakers' grasp, some of it is something that they cannot control and just have to react to. So what I am going to present to you today is a survey of our members and how they are currently dealing with the current situation in terms of retirement savings and the role of financial education within that.

I am going to give you an overview of the paper that we are currently working on. I will try to summarize key findings, but obviously as this is still work in progress, you may feel that there are other things and if you do feel that there is something that should be added, I would love to hear about it because then we can talk together within the expert group and within our network and actually develop this paper further. The idea is that once we have sufficient evidence, we will be able to work toward both guiding policy and also a very practical toolkit. There are already some that exist, as I will show you later, but we want to really build on those to be as practical and as up-to-date as we possibly can. I will also tell you what the next steps will be for the OECD and how you may be involved in that.

First of all, we surveyed the countries in 2014. We have over 100 countries within the international network, so we have a lot of countries. Of those, 24 responded, while two countries said they actually really did not have enough information about the role of financial education in their countries to give us some important answers. I know for a fact there are people not just in the audience, but even here on the stage that have not yet answered this questionnaire. So if you are one of them and you would like to, please do. It is really important when we are trying to draw together good practices that we actually hear from everybody. It is equally important that we hear about challenges as well as solutions, because if we do not know what the challenges are, we cannot possibly try to help you to identify solutions.

So what did we find out? Well, first of all, we asked within the questionnaire about some of the challenges in terms of how much personal responsibility people actually have, because if the state takes all the responsibility, then perhaps there is not much of a role for financial education. But not surprisingly, we found there are varied but increasing levels of personal responsibility in most countries. At the most basic level, state pension rarely gives people the standard of living that they really would hope for in retirement. So one of the most basic responsibilities that people actually have is to find out whether or not they will have sufficient money. Then, working from that, how much in contributions they should be making to their pensions.

Then there are also issues within some countries about the retirement age and actually understanding the impact of the retirement age. So if the compulsory retirement age is relatively low, understanding that means you have fewer years in which you will be saving and so your retirement pot will be suffering as a result. There are also issues in some countries about how people receive their retirement funds, whether they get a lump sum or whether they are expected to choose an annuity, and this is happening with state pensions as well as with private pensions.

Some other challenges that we identified across countries were understanding default options and auto-enrollment. These are tools that are actually developed to try to help people to save for their retirement. But nevertheless, it is recognized by policymakers that you need to understand what these are doing to you and whether the default is right for you or whether auto-enrollment is the most appropriate choice for you at this time.

People need to understand how much to invest in their own private pensions or how much to invest in defined contribution pensions, certainly. Also, sometimes, in some countries, they actually get a choice of where to invest, so making the investment decision for themselves, or a choice of how much and when to draw out and how to use the money. These are just some of the issues we came across in the questionnaire results.

But one of the other big issues that I have not listed here is that people's retirement funds often include a variety of different products and one of the most complicated things that people have to do is to try to have an overview of their own situation. They may have worked in various different jobs and have various different pensions as a result, on top of their state pension, on top of savings, possibly on top of a property that they intend to sell. So actually, as well as these different challenges posed by different pension systems and different pensions approaches, the general challenge of just managing your own life and knowing exactly what you have, and remembering that, for some people, they may have these in different countries across different situations, for example. There are various ways in which their retirement fund can be extremely complicated.

Within our questionnaire we asked policymakers what they felt were the biggest challenges and I think two clear messages came out. The first is that people have this challenge of being able to try to forecast their own needs, recognizing that there is uncertainty, recognizing that their income may change throughout their life, that they may have different needs in older age from their current needs, but nevertheless, trying to be able to have a basic understanding of the risks they face, of the rewards they may be able to achieve, and how they should judge that. This does not necessarily mean that we are trying to create people who are extremely technically competent, but they need to know how far they can go themselves and when they may need help.

Also this issue that I mentioned before of the low and inadequate retirement income that is going to be a reality for so many people as they hit retirement; this is just a fact. It came out through the questionnaires that this is something that policymakers are particularly worried about. It was very interesting that it was the case even in countries where the state pension was relatively high compared to the standard of living, so it is actually an issue in almost all of the countries that responded to our survey.

At the same time, it seems that most countries have got some parts of their pension system sorted out, so that they are not too concerned. So, for example, in most of the countries that responded, there was actually what policymakers considered to be a sufficient choice of pension products, so it was not, in most cases, a problem of lack of suitable products. Interestingly, and maybe slightly more concerning, fewer than half of the countries that came back felt that there was a problem with getting appropriate advice. It is interesting that the advice may be there, but I think in a lot of cases people are not aware of how to access it or even how and when they should access it. So it is something that may exist, but we need to know a lot more about how it is being used and how well people understand what is available to them and also at what cost.

So, we know that financial education has a role, but it is not the only thing that has a role. We always talk about financial education as being a complement to other approaches. In terms of trying to increase personal retirement savings, the research has shown that auto-enrollment is being used increasingly to try to increase the take-up and use of pensions, along with designing new products that are simpler, that are easier for people to use, that are more accessible, and trying to broaden access by changing the criteria for paying into certain pensions. So some countries have done this on a voluntary basis, others have done it on a compulsory basis, but various different policy approaches just to try to shift the participation rate across the whole population.

But it is not enough just to try and increase take-up if people are not paying enough into their pensions, because they will still face the same problem in retirement. So the other policy approach that we are seeing over and over again is to find ways of trying to increase the amount of money that is getting paid in. That could be by forcing people to just simply pay more in, or it could be through incentivization, or it could be through making people work longer so that their working life is much, much longer than it used to be. The incentives we heard a little bit about already; some of them, for example, are tax incentives, some of them are matched funds. There are various ways that countries have tried to increase retirement savings outside of the realm of financial education.

In the questionnaire we asked countries to tell us about the role of financial education. There are some things that stand out in terms of how financial education can help people to understand the ways in which they can save for their own retirement. Actually, one of the messages that comes across is understanding how to apply the math that you may have learned in school to your personal finances, so understanding the importance of compound interest, understanding percentages. This is not something that comes out very strongly in some of the other financial education research, but it is so important for these complex decisions. Along with this, there are the classic messages of being able to budget so that people actually have some money left to save at the end of the month, or maybe at the beginning of the month, depending how they budget, making an informed decision. So the actual process of being able to gather information and compare and contrast.

Understanding the benefit of saving from a young age was identified as an important topic that should be addressed through financial education. We might think that the population tends not to think about retirement at a very young age, but it is clear that it is becoming increasingly important that they do so.

Knowing how to work out how much is enough: the idea is that people should have adequate savings for retirement, not that they should live in poverty throughout their working life, it is about getting the balance right. Policymakers recognize that even though it is a difficult topic, it is an important topic and balancing that with the last one, which is recognizing when you need additional retirement savings, recognizing how you might go about that. For some people that might not be a pension, it might be a different approach.

You may feel that some of those are slightly contradictory, but that is the process of collecting information from different countries, from different sources and one of the things that we do and that we will continue to do with the network is to work on prioritizing those and actually identifying why some countries have some priorities and why some countries have others. A lot of it is to do with the different stages or the different processes that are going on within their countries in terms of pensions.

So financial education is happening; we are not just talking about a wish list here, we are talking about things that are actually going on in countries, in two ways really. The first is, as you heard this morning, the national strategies, the strategic overarching approaches to try to improve the levels of financial education across populations. In some cases, this is part of financial inclusion, it is providing financial education in order to increase financial inclusion within a country. In Nigeria, for example, pension projects are considered to be an important part of that process of talking about financial inclusion, financial education, and saving for retirement.

The other overarching broad financial education that is of relevance to retirement saving, though not necessarily designed specifically for that, is financial education in schools. Again, you heard a lot about that this morning and it is broadly recognized that if we do want people to save from a young age, then they need to understand why that is happening.

Also, in a lot of countries where even from their first job young people will be auto-enrolled or they will be in a system where they are expected to pay into their pension, it can help them if they can understand why that process is in place and the benefits of staying in and not actually withdrawing from that, in most cases.

But then we also found that some countries have got very specific programs that are designed for retirement planning in particular. Sometimes these are also happening within a national strategy, but sometimes they are happening outside, they are designed specifically because there has been a policy change and policymakers are wanting to inform and educate their population about these changes. So sometimes these are actually aimed at the whole population and making sure that everybody is informed. Other times it is about identifying particular target groups that are perhaps not saving enough for retirement and working with those and finding ways of educating those.

Because there are different needs and also different approaches to providing financial education, it is not surprising that there are different delivery methods. But one of the things that really stands out when you talk about financial education for long-term savings or for retirement savings is that it quite often needs to occur at a national level, because really the savings level across the population is a problem. So you see these national level tools such as awareness campaigns, perhaps through the media, online tools; these are very, very important. But they are not the only things that matter. Online tools are really good because they take away that important challenge that we talked about earlier, which is the math. So if you have online tools, the tool has the math and computing power inside it, so the individual can concentrate on the outcomes. But workshops and seminars, working within the workplace in countries where most people are in the formal sector, are also really beneficial and a lot of countries told us that is what they do. Also trying innovative and trying to find new ways of creating new financial education approaches has been found to be effective.

We have a session later on target groups, so I will not go into this in much detail, but I do not think it will surprise you to see that the vast majority of countries, if they have particular target groups, are looking at young people, women, and pre-retirees. Some other target groups that were mentioned in the responses to our questionnaire were various different types of vulnerable groups, people who are job-seeking, so not yet necessarily paying into a pension, and people who have got new financial priorities because their children have left home.

Those were the summaries. The next part of my presentation, which is going to be very short for now, is what we hope to do with this information and any additional information that you can provide to us. We want to build on existing OECD policy tools, so these are policy tools that help policymakers to consider the issues and to identify the solutions that we are aware of. We are building at the moment on three sets of tools that were created in 2005, 2008, and 2012, and I am sure you will appreciate there is a vast amount of information that we have now that we did not have then and countries have got a vast amount of experience now that they did not have then. There has also been a financial crisis in that time, so there are a lot of reasons why it is worth going back and looking at these.

We recognize that one of the things we need to work on more is to look at the needs of particular target groups. Again, if you have any information about how you are using financial education with particular target groups, please do let us know. You do not need to fill in a complete questionnaire, if you could just provide us with information bilaterally, that would be great. Also the fact that we know that pension systems are changing dramatically and so anything that we can add into our policy tools to help countries to work with their population as things change is, we believe, an important addition to this revised tool. But alongside the policy tools, we also recognize that there is a need for practical tools, for a matrix to explain to people if you have this kind of pension system, then why not use this kind of financial education. So we are also working on developing and updating existing practical tools in order to do that.

Our intention is that we will add as many countries as we possibly can to this report. We will really draw out additional findings. The questionnaire is much more detailed than I have been able to present today and there is a lot of information that we can add to what we already know before we start to work on the policy tools. So by May, when we have our next International Network on Financial Education meetings, we will hopefully have a draft report that will represent as many countries as possible and then through the following months to October, we hope to work on these policy tools and practical tools so that by next year, these will be available for you to use, they will be in the public domain, and they will be there for you to apply and also for you to feed back to us on how efficient and effective they have been.

I am going to stop there, please do look out for myself or for Ms. Messy, tell us anything you can about financial education for retirement savings and if you do not have the opportunity to do that, an e-mail would be great. We really would like to know more and make this paper as relevant and practical as possible. Thank you.

Prof. Elsa Fornero: Thank you very much, Dr. Atkinson. Thank you for providing a very interesting and comprehensive survey. I am sure there will be many questions. I have a very quick one, just yes or no. Is there also a ranking of countries in terms of financial education and effectiveness of pension policies or provisions?

Dr. Adele Atkinson: No. I could give a much more detailed answer.

Prof. Elsa Fornero: I am firmly convinced that financial literacy is an essential feature also for the effectiveness of pension reforms, so I believe this will be the subject of future research and I will take part in this effort. Now let us move to the second panelist, Ms. Anna Zelentsova, whose topic is how to provide effective financial education for pension management in the Russian Federation. Please, Anna.

Addressing the Challenges of Providing Effective Financial Education for Pension Management in the Russian Federation

Anna Zelentsova, Head of Financial Literacy at Ministry of Finance, co-chair of the Global Partnership on Financial Inclusion: Thank you very much and good afternoon. I am very glad to be here with you, my first time in Tokyo, so thank you very much to the organizers for inviting me. It is my pleasure to be here and delve a bit more into the Russian experience, though as you rightly mentioned, there are a lot of challenges in financial education and especially in retirement. Still, we need to work on solutions, but I will provide you with some, our ideas about progress in financial education in the Russian Federation.

But first just a little bit of background on financial literacy in the Russian Federation to understand in which environment we are and what is the level of financial literacy of the general population, the adult population. I do not talk here about young people, even though we also participated in the PISA survey. We are in the middle of the ranking, between France and the US. Regarding young people, I think we are more optimistic about them, but of course the adult population did not have the experience of being responsible for their own finances. Under the Soviet system, pensions were provided by the government, so people did not need to make their own choices, to be responsible for them, though the level of savings was higher. So still the culture of savings is more for older people, for pensioners in the Russian Federation, and young people of course like to consume more. They want to buy something new just now, not save for their future, so there are some mixed cultural factors.

It is typical that people do not trust financial institutions, yet they do use them. They take credit and various financial products, but only one-fifth think that if there were any financial disputes, any problems with the financial institutions, they would be resolved fairly. That is why it is a big task for us to improve the trust of people in the financial system and financial organizations. Of course, in parallel, there needs to be improvement in behavior of these financial organizations, financial institutions.

There is a low level of savings among the population. Our own recent national survey shows that half of the population does not save at all. Many people still keep money under the pillow and this is not good for long-term savings and for investment in the economy. Less than 40% actually recognize their responsibility for their own financial decisions. If we speak about investments, they say "if I lose from my investments or if I buy an apartment and the price of the apartment goes down, the government should return the money to me." So again this is quite a mixed understanding of responsibilities and rights. While 67% of Russian people are not financially literate, it is quite a good result that 66% of the population understands the risk/reward principle, which is also important for investments and for long-term savings.

This is the context. And regarding the pension system itself, just like many other countries, we are in process of reform. Our reforms have been under way for more than 10 years. The process started in 2002, and from this year, from 1 January 2015, the new pension system formally came into effect. It is really new, so thanks for inviting me to speak about it. This way I was able to learn more about it myself, as it is quite complicated. I will not give you all the details—it would take too long—but I will just tell you what is important and what factors affect the pension size. First, the level of official (stated) salary in the Russian Federation is still quite a big grey area, especially in small businesses or self-employment. These people do not pay taxes, do not pay social payments, because the official level of their salary is lower than the real level. This is very important.

Second, what is important is the age at which people decide to take this money to officially claim a pension. The current pension age is 55 years for women and 60 years for men, but you can continue to work; it is not compulsory, you can continue to work and you can start to take your pension later, in which case it will be much higher. But there are also debates on increasing the pension age. Life expectancy in the Russian Federation, unfortunately, is not as high as in Japan, especially for men. Yet, there are debates that especially for women, with higher life expectancies than men, 55 years is probably too early for the economy to go on pension. So there are public debates now.

One more important thing is that even though the pension system is compulsory and employers contribute to the insurance of every employee, within this compulsory system, those below the age of 43 years since 1 January have had the choice to go only for the compulsory pension or instead to allocate some percentage of this employer contribution to a nongovernment pension fund. So there is now a small choice, an opportunity for people to make their own decision and manage their own savings. However, the pension funds and the central bank do not provide much incentive because of high inflation; it is better to stay within the compulsory scheme as it will cover inflation in any case, but you cannot guarantee this with other investment funds.

These are just a few features to show that the current system is quite complicated and ordinary people without financial education cannot always understand it. Apart from that, as I said, there is low trust in financial institutions, private pension funds, and other investment funds. And for those people who rely only on the compulsory public scheme, if their salary is low and if they do not work for many years, their public pension will be very low and will be insufficient to maintain their standard of living. So the dilemma is how to deal with it.

When we ask people in national social surveys, do you know that public pension payments benefits will not be enough for you to live the life you have gotten used, they say yes—70% of people say yes, they understand it. Then we ask what are you going to do with it and this is a more difficult question. When we ask people what kind of retirement strategies they have, not many of them want to use or know how to use the different financial instruments for that. Most of them say that they will work harder, they will continue to work, or find other ways (Table 2.1).

Table 2.1   Retirement strategies of population: Different instruments and ways to live on retirement

Do you plan any other sources of income when you retire besides the public pension benefits?	%
I will continue to work when I achieve retirement age or find another suitable job.	42
No, I do not plan any additional sources of income, only public pension.	25
I believe my children will help me.	12
I will grow vegetables, fruits in my country house.	12
I plan to use my savings which I am going to do through pension funds.	**11**
I hope to receive additional payments from the government.	9
I hope my spouse will continue to work on pension and we will use this money.	8
I do not know yet, I will think about it when this time comes.	6
I will move to a cheaper flat and will use this money.	3
I hope that charity would help me.	2
Additionally to the pension payments I will get income from the flat rent, investments.	**2**
I hope for money from my family, succession.	2
Other	2

Source: NAFI (2013).

We at the Ministry of Finance, together with the World Bank, started a national project, and within this project we developed financial education programs for different target groups and so we have this wider financial education, but we have also more specific education, specific to the retirement issues. We have distant online education seminars, workshops, and different types of self-learning. We also have different types of brochures for different ages.

In November we had our first national savings week, which was mostly about savings and retirement. We got very good media coverage, which we had not expected—all federal channels did interviews and featured the savings week. That is why we liked this idea, but this year we want to start a big public information campaign and go nationwide. For this we will use different channels, depending on the age groups we are targeting; online information portals, etc. What we learned from savings week is that we need to know better what channels to use and what messages people want to hear and will make use of. We had thought that working adults do not go to seminars, they prefer to access information online. But they did come to our seminars, saying they found it easier to find time one day to go and listen rather than to read about it themselves. So our earlier stereotypes were destroyed during this pilot program.

That is all. I hope I managed the time.

Prof. Elsa Fornero: A very short time for such a large and complex country starting a new path of learning.

Ms. Anna Zelentsova: It is true. Yes.

Prof. Elsa Fornero: Well, I visited as an expert for the World Bank during the time of the first pension reform. I had really the feeling that for many people managing money was something new. Certainly, the trust in financial markets was very, very low. At that time the financial crisis was still fresh in people's memory. Thank you very much for this interesting presentation.

Ms. Anna Zelentsova: Thank you very much.

Prof. Elsa Fornero: It is now the turn of Dr. Julie Agnew. She will talk about personal pension investments and the role of financial literacy. So we move to a country that is financially sophisticated and where financial education is possibly also a problem.

Personal Pension Investments and the Role of Financial Literacy

Julie Agnew, Director of Boehly Center for Excellence in Finance, Mason School of Business, US: It is a pleasure to be here and I would like to thank the organizers. I have learned a great deal so far this morning and today I am here to share with you a little bit about the US experience, specifically what we have learned in the pension area and why financial literacy and financial education are very important.

Before I begin, I want to provide context for what has been happening in pensions in the US. Now, if you look at Figure 2.1, you will see several

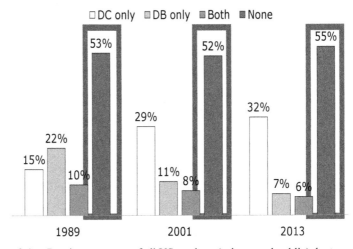

Figure 2.1   Pension coverage of all US workers (private and public), by type of plan

Source: Center for Retirement Research at Boston College website. CRR staff estimates based on US Board of Governors of the Federal Reserve System, 1989–2013 Survey of Consumer Finances (accessed 13 January 2015). http://crr.bc.edu/wp-content/uploads/1012/01/Pension-coverage1.pdf

different decades. The far right column in each cluster displays the percentage of all workers, both in the government and in private industry, who do not have any pension coverage. This percentage has been relatively stable, with a little over half of employees without any pension coverage at all.

What has changed, though, is the distribution of those people that do have pension coverage (Figure 2.2). You can see that the defined contribution only piece actually increased over the years—it was only 15% in 1989 and rose to 32% in 2013. On the other hand, those that have defined benefit plans, which are quite easy for individuals to manage because all they have to do is go to work, allow an expert to make all the difficult financial decisions in the plan, and when they retire, accept a check until they die; these types of plans now are really becoming a thing of the past.

The consequence of this shift is that people are faced with very complicated decisions, a recurring theme in all the preceding presentations. Participants in DC plans have to think about asset allocation. In some government plans, participants actually have to decide between the DC plan and the DB plan offered to them, resulting in an extremely complicated discussion. It was also mentioned earlier today that distribution decisions,

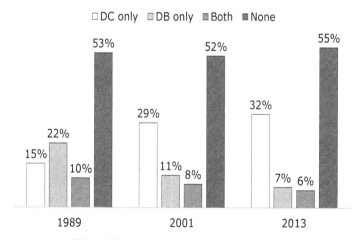

Figure 2.2   Percentage in DC plans increasing

Source: Center for Retirement Research at Boston College website. CRR staff estimates based on US Board of Governors of the Federal Reserve System, 1989–2013 Survey of Consumer Finances (accessed 13 January 2015). http://crr.bc.edu/wp-content/uploads/1012/01/Pension-coverage1.pdf

such as annuity versus lump sum choices and life term estimations, are increasingly difficult choices people must make.

Regarding financial literacy, despite some false impressions that US citizens are highly financially sophisticated, we face many challenges in the US in this area. In addition, literature exists showing that there is a relationship between making mistakes in pension plans and low financial literacy. There are also benefits from financial sophistication. For example, a new study by Clark, Lusardi, and Mitchell (2014) finds that those who have higher returns in their defined contribution plans are those who are financially sophisticated.

Another point of focus in the pension discussion is knowledge of pension features. Individuals may know the difference between a stock and a bond, but if they do not understand the features and incentives of their pension plans, they are not going to respond correctly to them. One important feature in many defined contribution plans in the US is an employer match. For employer matches, if the employee makes a contribution, the employer matches that contribution to a certain extent. Well, the research demonstrates that if you as a participant are unaware that there is a match, you are less likely to contribute and receive that match. We undertook a project using administrative data and tied survey responses to it, and we found exactly that. People were less likely to participate in plans when they were not aware that there was a match.

Another really interesting paper by Brown and Weisbenner (2014) used administrative data combined with survey data. They found that that if employees' understanding of their plan's features is correct, employees are making sound decisions. However, the problem is when you ask employees what they believe about the plan, their understanding is inaccurate, so they actually are making poor choices. Therefore, while it is important that individuals understand compounding and different asset classes, they must also know the features of their plan.

Another important issue is how people feel about retirement decisions and there is a bit of a disturbing picture, but it comes from discussions with real employees. When I conduct research, I find it very useful not only to look at the administrative data, but also to talk to the people involved in the plan. During focus groups on retirement decisions, we asked individuals, as a warm-up exercise, to pick from an array of different pictures and choose those that depicted how they felt when they were thinking about retirement decisions. We provided pictures of hammocks on beaches, beautiful sunsets, and other happy things, as well as some darker images. What is disturbing is that the picture that was chosen most often was that of a man who looks like he is just about to get cut while he is being shaved. The following are quotes from people as to why they chose this picture. One person said, "I feel totally powerless when I am thinking about my decisions." Another person said, "how the shave turns out is completely out of my control"; he was drawing a parallel between the shave and his retirement savings. Then finally someone said, "I cannot tell which choices are right and which choices are wrong. I would like to understand what is going on, but I just don't." This is where financial education is important because when people are feeling overwhelmed, our research shows that many experience information overload and they do nothing in response.

There is much we academic researchers can study to improve pension experiences. All of these different cogs in the machine that academics are focusing on: Can we design the plan more effectively so that people make good decisions? Can we communicate better? Can we use behavioral psychology to help people do the right thing?

Now, regarding choice architecture, a lot of people say, well if you just design a pension plan well, you can disregard financial education. One of the most popular design features today is automatic enrollment and you have probably seen these impressive statistics (Choi et al. 2006). This famous study showed that in a corporation, before employees were automatically enrolled, meaning they had to voluntarily join, there were very low participation rates. When the plan switched to automatic enrollment, such that participants were enrolled first having to quit if they did not want to participate, participation rates changed dramatically; but if people are rational, the participation numbers should be exactly the same. This is a great success, and I have attended conferences where people say, with design features like this there is no need to spend any money on financial education.

The problem, however, as reported in the *Wall Street Journal* (Tergesen 2011) and found in academic research, is that there is a default bias in contribution levels. As a result, when plans automatically enroll people, they often enroll them at a very low savings rate and employees stay at that rate. When researchers looked at the data, they found that, while overall savings in the plan increased, the employees who normally would have voluntarily joined actually saved at lower rates than they would have chosen for themselves. So that is a consequence to bear in mind.

Another consequence that is not discussed that often is that there can be regret when participants do not understand their decisions. For example, there was a study looking at how people in government plans choose between different types of plans they are offered (Brown, Farrell, and Weisbenner 2011). The default for these employees was a DB plan. The study found that the highest amount of regret experienced by employees was for those that actually were defaulted into the DB plan. On the contrary, those who reported in the survey that they actively chose the DB plan experienced much less regret. Therefore, understanding the default is very important.

Now who defaults? We conducted an experimental study where people had to choose asset allocations and a default asset allocation was set. We tested financial literacy and we found that the people who defaulted were more likely those with low financial literacy—20% defaulted with low financial literacy while only 2% defaulted with high financial literacy. This is supported by additional research. Referring back to the "which plan should I choose?" study that used administrative data, they also found that if employees had some basic knowledge or more advanced knowledge or understood the plan, they were less likely to default. But if the information was overwhelming to the employee, they were more likely to default.

As a result, some might say to just give everybody more information so they can better understand their options. We conducted a large-scale experiment where we put people through a game where they had to choose between an annuity and a lump sum. This is a pretty complicated decision for most individuals. In the game, after they made the choice, we had them live a simulated life making financial choices, and we observed how well they did after six periods. We found that those who experienced that information overload when learning about the their choices were 30% less likely to feel confident when they were making those decisions. Subjects were informed about how much money they made after they played the game, and even if they made a lot of money they were less likely to report satisfaction with their decision when the game was complete if they experienced information overload. Again, financial literacy is key, as those with low financial literacy are more likely to experience information overload, another reason why we have to keep this in mind.

I spent 2012 in Australia and my co-authors and I were looking at how people use financial advisers. Some argue that we should just send participants to a financial adviser and let the advisors make the participants' choices. We were testing whether credentials mattered. Well the unfortunate thing is we found that people could be easily manipulated, especially if they were presented a difficult piece of advice, and we found that people did look at credentials. When we used a real credential, subjects were more likely to choose the adviser with the credential, even in some cases when that adviser gave bad advice. We found it a little worrisome when we also tested whether people understood what the adviser credentials signified. Of the top three credentials chosen as trustworthy by subjects out of a large list, two were fake credentials that people thought were the best credentials to have. In the US, this is a problem because there are over 100 different credentials that people can have. So the outstanding question, to which I do not yet have the answer is this: Could financial literacy and education also help in this case by making one less susceptible to manipulation and more aware of what the credentials mean?

So my bottom line is, financial education is important—no matter how well designed your plan is, you need financial education. So what kind of financial education is available in the US? There was a survey done by the Plan Sponsor Council of America (PSCA) that revealed what types of education private plans were reporting they offered (Table 2.2). The most popular were enrollment kits, also e-mails were very popular,

Table 2.2 Financial education in sample of US DC private plans

Most Common Type of Education Approaches		Most Common Primary Reason for Providing Plan Education	
1. Enrollment kit	(63.3%)	1. Increase participation	(25.5%)
2. E-mail	(60.3%)	2. Retirement planning	(20.2%)
3. Internet/Intranet sites	(57.4%)	3. Increase deferrals	(16.1%)
4. Fund performance sheets	(43.4%)	4. Increase appreciation for	
5. Seminars/Workshops	(41.2%)	the plan	(14.8%)
54% of plans evaluate the success of education programs.			

Source: PSCA (2014).

and seminars—about 41% of the plans gave seminars. The goals of the education programs were good, like increasing participation, increasing deferrals, or simply increasing the appreciation of the plan.

Now the kicker is, only 54% of these plans actually evaluated their education programs. They were spending all this money on education, but they were not checking if it worked. I want to argue that efficacy is the most important consideration, and I know that lots of people agree with me after watching the earlier presentations today. Results from Choi et al. (2002) demonstrate why evaluation is important. In their study, a corporation held an education seminar telling employees about a retirement plan they could join. Everyone that was not a member said "I am joining the plan," that is, 100% of those who responded in the survey afterward. Now think how many people actually joined the plan? In fact, only 14% later joined the plan; 47% said they were going to change their funds, but only 15% did; 36% said they would change their allocation, yet only 10% did. So you cannot just rely on these post-education surveys administered right after the seminar is over because everybody feels really great after those seminars. Then employees go home. They might have kids to attend to, work, or other matters that cause them to just never get around to doing what they said they were going to do.

We fielded a national survey of government retirement plans and we asked them, if they tested success, how do they do it (Figure 2.3)? What is a little alarming is that most of the plans just fielded the surveys right after the seminar or they said, "Oh, 10 people, 15 people showed up, this is great, it was a success." More importantly, only a minority used the methods that I think are better, which are testing actual investment behavior following the education.

So I have some tips for everybody, based on the US experience. First, when thinking about financial literacy, ensure the financial education programs encompass a broad scope of topics when you are thinking about retirement plans. You must educate participants about the features of the pension so that they can take advantage of the benefits. The second tip is my point about financial literacy being important no matter how well designed the plan. I am a champion of plan design, I do believe in the effectiveness of choice architecture and automatic enrollment, but I also think people need to be aware to help them to not become overwhelmed.

National Public Pension Plan Financial Education Survey 2012

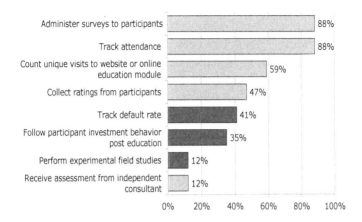

Figure 2.3   Some methods for measuring success in US government plans

Note: 21 DC and hybrid plans representing 80% of the 25 possible. These figures are based on 17 plans that measure success.
Source: Agnew and Hurwitz (2013).

There are potential unexpected consequences associated with some of the non-education solutions—defaults, communication, and financial advisers, and information overload—and education might help people avoid them. When we held our focus groups, many people basically told us, "I started thinking about retirement when I was young, I became overwhelmed and I just said I am not going to do anything." When they spoke to us they were in their 50s and 60s now facing difficult situations because of their earlier inaction. Hence, you do not want people to become overwhelmed early on, and education might help.

Third, I advise you to carefully evaluate education programs. You want to look at what participants actually do, not what their intentions are. I would advocate, as do many academics, thinking about evaluating programs like the healthcare industry conducts medical research. When they are testing a new drug, they would use control groups to see what really works. This method, like those we are implementing in a few studies right now (one in Australia), employs randomized controlled experiments, which are the right way to test whether an intervention is working or not.

If these experiments are something you might not be familiar with, there are many academics who would be quite willing, for free, to analyze the results if you let them publish them. Those are my three tips. Thanks.

Prof. Elsa Fornero: Thank you very much, Ms. Agnew. The polemics between those who stress the design in financial education and those who stress the importance of default mechanisms such as nudging are quite strange to me. I never understood the polemics that, let us say, some scholars, great scholars, have against financial education exactly because they think that designing "nice" default options is much more useful, which I think is simply not true. They seem to believe there is a substitution, either one or the other. To me there is a clear complementarity. You can have default options and they work better if people are financially literate.

Dr. Julie Agnew: Absolutely, yes and I think one of the other issues is that you learn from experience. If everyone is defaulted into their plans, then when you get older, you have had no market experience. Now you are older, you might have cognitive decline and you have to make some of the most difficult financial decisions you will ever face. So education, especially if you are not learning from experience, is important.

Prof. Elsa Fornero: This is certainly true. It is time for us to move to Australia, another large and very interesting country. Now I introduce Miles Larbey, a senior executive leader of Financial Literacy in ASIC, the Australian Securities and Investments Commission. Mr. Larbey, you have the floor.

The Role of Financial Education to Support Effective Pension Management in Australia

Miles Larbey, Senior Executive Leader, Financial Literacy, Australian Securities and Investments Commission (ASIC): Well thank you very much. It is my pleasure to be here this afternoon and talk a little bit about the Australian experience, both in terms of our retirement savings landscape and a bit about what we are doing at the Australian Securities and Investments Commission (ASIC) in terms of trying to help people make their choices through financial education. I would like to thank the ADBI and the OECD of course for hosting this conference and for inviting me to speak here today.

For those who do not know, ASIC is the equivalent of the Japan FSA. We are the financial conduct regulator for all types of financial products and services in Australia, including retirement savings and insurance. As part of our role to protect consumers of financial services, we are responsible for financial literacy in Australia at a government level. We are, as part of that, responsible for leading and coordinating Australia's national financial literacy strategy and, as we heard earlier, in Australia we are actually onto our second national strategy, which was released recently.

This strategy is built around a number of strategic priorities—and I did bring a few copies, but you can access it online of course if you are interested—including trying to provide guidance and support for particular target groups in the population or focus in particular areas. One of those target groups is pre-retirees and retirees and the whole concept of long-term planning for retirement is a key part of the national financial literacy strategy.

I think we have heard from a few speakers today how in many countries populations are aging and this is certainly the case in Australia and, as we have heard, that is obviously a very good thing on the one hand, but represents challenges on the other. By 2040, the estimated life expectancy for a man in Australia will be 86 years and 89 years for a woman. That does mean we need to think about retirement savings or a system of retirement savings that allows for resources to last longer to take account of these increased life expectancies.

I thought I might just spend a minute to talk about the retirement planning framework in Australia, which is different to other countries. It is built around three pillars. Firstly, we have an aged pension, which is available from the government for anyone who qualifies on a means-tested basis. In other words, there is a test for level of income or assets, and if an Australian does not have those levels of income or assets, then they can access an aged pension through the social security system. It is an important safety net. I think it is about A$25,000 per year for a single person and I think still more than 80% of Australian retirees access some form of aged pension.

The second pillar of our system is, and this might be where we differ from some other countries, we have compulsory what we call superannuation, retirement savings that accumulate while people are in the workforce. Almost every Australian worker is required to participate in a superannuation scheme, retirement savings scheme, while they are in the workforce. This system was introduced in 1992 and I do not suppose the term behavioral economics or default settings in financial products were even talked about in those days, but the policymakers, without realizing it, were implementing a significant behavioral economics or default based system whereby everybody would have a proportion of their salary paid into a retirement savings product. It is currently 9.5% of salary and that will move up to 12% over a number of years. This contribution is paid by the employer, it is taxed at a concessional rate. The concessionally taxed part of it, capped up to A$30,000 per year, can be put into this compulsory superannuation. It means, as I said, every working adult Australian has, or most working adult Australians have, got some superannuation savings. Obviously as younger generations come through and benefit from that throughout their entire working life, it does provide a good basis.

But it does not come free of challenges. The fact that it is compulsory, in a way, increases the onus to make sure people understand what is happening with their money. People have to make choices in this system, they have to choose their fund, they have to choose how the money is invested and in a way, Australian workers—given that these funds are overwhelmingly defined contribution funds—participate in the financial markets as retail investors, whether they like it or not, whether they are equipped to do that or not. Certainly at ASIC and across the industry, we think that comes with the onus and responsibility to provide education for people about how to manage this.

Of course lastly, the final pillar of our retirement savings framework is voluntary savings. People can of course save for their retirement in whatever format they want. They can make additional contributions into their superannuation fund and we know that about 14% of Australians do that, or they can save in some other way and many people do that through property or other forms of savings.

Box 2.1   Superannuation facts and figures

As at 30 June 2013, A$1.62 trillion in superannuation assets (APRA) held in the following types of superannuation fund:

- Retail funds
- Industry funds
- Public sector funds
- Corporate funds
- Self-managed superannuation funds (SMSF)—509,362 funds at June 2013

Superannuation contributions to June 2013 totaled A$115.3 billion (APRA)

Average superannuation balance at time of retirement in 2011/12, A$197,000 for men and A$105,000 for women (ASFA)

Men held around 64% of total account balances in 2011/12, compared to 36% for women (ASFA)

Source: ASIC.

Partly because of that compulsory superannuation that has been in existence since 1992, Australia now has one of the world's largest pools of retirement savings at A$1.6 trillion at the end of 2013 financial year. I think it is now about A$1.8 trillion, which is more than the gross domestic product (GDP) of Australia, so it is a very, very significant amount of money when you consider the size of the Australian population and the fact that I think our economy is about 12th. What this enormous amount of money means is that, at the moment, the average balance for people retiring, as I say, these figures are a bit dated now, is nearly A$200,000 for men and A$100,000 for women. So there are differences certainly in terms of how the genders participate in the superannuation system. As you can see here, men hold about two-thirds of the superannuation balances compared to women (Box 2.1).

Alright, so as I said, this pot of superannuation savings, while it is very positive in many respects, does come with challenges. There are continuing low levels of engagement among the population. Only about a third of people could tell you what their superannuation balance is. As I said, the compulsory nature of this scheme means people are responsible for potentially complex decisions around where to invest the money, which fund to choose, make decisions around fees, and so on. People are, of course, responsible for their allocation decisions, and, as people age, they have to make such decisions, particularly people coming up for retirement. Of course the risk of making a bad decision is significantly enhanced then because you do not then have a whole working life to go back and recover those savings. There is a lack of awareness of how much people would need in retirement. We know that only about one-fifth of Australians have a long-term financial plan. Knowing what your budget is going to look like in retirement is obviously something that is difficult for people.

At ASIC we have tried to address some of these issues through financial education in a number of ways. Our financial literacy program is called ASIC's MoneySmart and the flagship product there is our website and this is just a screenshot of the website. But essentially what we do through financial education in this area is try and provide people with dedicated, real life, accessible information around their rights and responsibilities for superannuation, understanding investment options and strategies. We try and provide people with a range of online tools and I will show you a couple of examples there and the idea of these is to try and make information more engaging, more interactive, more personalized, more relevant to people (Figure 2.4).

We have a number of tools, which are very popular, specifically in relation to retirement decisions. One is this retirement planner, picking up on what I was saying about people not understanding how much money they might need or where that money might come from. This tool actually allows people to see how much income they will have and from different sources and, more importantly, the impact of different choices that they might make now as to what that future income will look like. It allows people to test different scenarios and hopefully get more informed in terms of making decisions in relation to their retirement savings.

Similarly, we have an online calculator that tells people how much balance they can expect to have in their superannuation account after a certain number of years, depending on different levels of fees, and it provides people with simple tips and action points if they do not like the results (Figure 2.5). So for example, obviously shopping around for a fund with a lower level of fees might be one very obvious sort of action that people can take.

Figure 2.4 Retirement planner

Source: ASIC's MoneySmart website (https://www.moneysmart.gov.au/tools-and-resources/calculators-and-apps/retirement-planner).

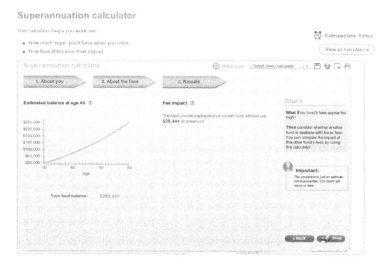

Figure 2.5 Superannuation calculator

Source: ASIC's MoneySmart website (https://www.moneysmart.gov.au/tools-and-resources/calculators-and-apps/superannuation-calculator).

One thing that is interesting about this calculator and something that we found has worked very well is that financial institutions are required to provide a link to this calculator with their disclosure documents. We know from behavioral insights and economics that providing information just in time or at the point of decision-making is very effective. So that is actually quite a neat way, I think, of working with industry in complement to the regulatory system in terms of trying to use financial education to help people make choices.

Now I am very, very conscious of time. Just lastly, we work very closely with other government agencies to run seminars for people about planning for retirement. This is a series of national, free seminars, which is run through our social security department. At ASIC we provide content and we train the people doing it and I should note that the financial services industry themselves do make a significant effort, or at least many of them do, to try and improve the engagement of the members of the super funds and they do that through a range of different ways.

That is just a very quick snapshot of what we are doing in Australia. Thank you.

Prof. Elsa Fornero: Thank you very much for your retirement planner. I can say that in this way practice is starting to interact with theory, an appropriate close to a very interesting session. Wrapping up, I just want to touch very briefly on some issues that we have discussed and that, in my opinion, will certainly be of general interest.

First, we have extensively examined financial literacy from a retirement savings and pensions angle, but we might not have sufficiently specified whether general financial literacy is sufficient for pension decisions or whether some pension-specific financial literacy issues should be included in financial literacy programs. I will give you an example: we say that people must have a general idea of risk diversification. Is there something specific that people should know when investing money for retirement?

Second, there is a growing world shift—which started in Europe and the US and expanded far and wide to countries such as the Russian Federation and Australia—away from what has generally been known as the "defined benefit" system. People were granted a replacement ratio, which was a very, very nice feature in a pension system: you knew for certain, from the start, what percentage of your final salary your pension would amount to. In Italy, a 40-year long working life would get you 80% of your final salary (or, in other versions, of the average monthly salary of your final three years at work). At present, most countries are, totally or partially switching to a DC, or defined contribution system. So how high will my pension be? It depends. It depends on so many factors. Of course, people are perplexed and many times experts have different opinions on how much of this complicated DC mechanism should become common knowledge. Otherwise said, how much responsibility about an individual's pension should be passed down to the individual herself.

Third, we have discussed ways of providing financial education programs, policy tools, and so on. We have seen that there are different stages in this provision of financial education, different ways of looking at the effectiveness of programs. This means that, at OECD and elsewhere, there is still a lot of work to do, we are still at the initial stage of what for many researchers will be a lifelong program.

But now, your questions; you have many perhaps and so I would like to give the floor to you. Please.

Open Floor Discussion

Peter Morgan, Senior Consultant for Research, ADBI: Thanks very much for very interesting presentations. I am just wondering, given that now presumably there is some track record of people's experience in managing their own DC type plans, has there been any work on how people have performed actually and how that might relate to their background in terms of education, that sort of thing?

Prof. Elsa Fornero: In terms of investment?

Dr. Peter Morgan: Yes, how have their self-investments performed?

Dr. Julie Agnew: There is actually a new study that came out last year by Bob Clark, Annamaria Lusardi, and Olivia Mitchell (2014), that looked at the excess return in DC plans and they found more financially sophisticated people had higher returns. So there is new evidence coming out that they do do better. But this highlights why analyzing the right kind of data is so important. If you have the administrative data to measure the returns, you also need the survey evidence.

Prof. Elsa Fornero: According to the new results that you quoted, it would seem that financial literacy, or rather financial knowledge more than literacy, has contributed quite a lot to income distribution and income inequality. So if an individual is rich, she is likely to be more financially knowledgeable and in consequence will receive higher earnings, including pension, on her wealth. There is a positive circle for the individual, but it might turn into a problem for society since we already have a very uneven wealth distribution.

But of course you were asking about DC and I think DC pension plans are relatively new. To my knowledge, and generally confining myself to Europe, I am not aware that there has been published research providing evidence on the effects of financial education on DC investments. I think it likely that the first ones will come from the Netherlands since the Dutch are massively switching from DB to DC and have also introduced massive financial education programs.

Mr. Miles Larbey: No, I am not aware of any studies on that specifically from Australia, I think partly because the pension sector is constantly undergoing innovation and change. In fact, a lot of work is now going on to build default settings for investment strategies over the lifetime of someone's membership in a fund, which might suggest that policymakers are not leaving it to investors to make those decisions.

Prof. Elsa Fornero: Other questions? Yes, please.

Audience member: I am from Nepal. I have a very small query. When there are pension fund managers and the countries are very risk prone, the incentive to save for later life is very low. That is a psychological sort of fear and I wonder if any kind of financial education could be of help in that sort of situation? Probably the expert from the Russian Federation knows about savings evaporating overnight, about people's fear of losing their savings.

Ms. Anna Zelentsova: Thank you very much. It is really a very important and good question and it is part of debates also in the Russian Federation, how to do better, especially when there is a high rate of inflation and there are risks. Last December, we had this wave when people started to consume more, so it was likely to be the start of crisis and depression; rationally you should save because you can lose your job, etc. But people started consuming because they were not sure if the value of their money would be the same in future because the ruble went down. So they behaved emotionally and, as some experts say, not rationally. I think they behaved rationally, but it is a different type of rationality, I mean they have rationales for their behavior. Also this rationale can be wrong, this is another reason, but we need to always understand these reasons and use this understanding and communicate with people and explain. When we just say you behave wrongly or you do stupid things, it does not work in financial education. So I think it is very important to understand first, and when we understand it we can communicate.

Second, anyway they should save, even if there is a debate on whether it is better to spend or save, because still they are going to live on a pension. So still there is a need to have this money, these assets for pensions. This was a question we asked in our national survey. If you are going to live on a pension, if you are not going to die earlier, you need money. When you explain to people that it is a matter of their wellbeing, that it is not only yes you can lose more, you should find better, more effective options, how to save this money—and how to invest the money is another story. This is the question of financial instruments. But the option just to spend now means that you will not have any future assets anyway. So we tried to communicate, we tried first of all to understand the reasoning, the rationale behind it. We tried to communicate with people in the right way, but still it is a big question and I would be interested to hear what other experts have to say on that.

Dr. Julie Agnew: We did some research looking at how we could push people with communications to making one decision or another. It was actually that annuity paper we were looking at. Once again, I go to the healthcare literature where we got our ideas, because in healthcare they have done a lot of research on how to get people to do things that are not a lot of fun, like some medical tests that you can think about. They used different ways of communicating, one of which is called fear appeals. To get you to take a certain cancer test, they will show you some of the negative things that can happen if you do not. Sometimes, though, with certain age groups, that will not work as well. We did some research and we found that actually the fear appeals worked fairly well with the annuity decision, but with the savings decision, young people acted differently from older people. There is a lot more work that needs to be done in this area in terms of how you frame things to individuals in order to make them maybe think about saving when they are 22 and do not want to really think about that right now, but maybe get them in the right frame of mind that they will. So there is some research to be done in this area.

Prof. Elsa Fornero: I would like to add that the advice dimension should be faced. Who is giving advice? How independent is the advisor? In Italy and other European countries, it was quite common for workers to turn to trade unions for advice, given the trade unions' very important role in all aspects of labor relations. It was a question of trust. Workers generally trusted the representatives they had themselves elected and who had proved effective in many aspects of work relationships, so why not assume that they might be equally effective in matters of pension fund and pension investment management? Nowadays trade unions are losing credibility, like many other institutions and so they are no longer trusted. But then the question arises of who should take up that role, of who should provide advice.

Economists are inclined to think that people have rational expectations, look clearly far ahead into the future, and just as clearly know exactly what they want to achieve. Research has shown that this is simply not the case. When people are obliged to participate in social security schemes, they are used to little or no choice: they have to participate, the contribution rate is fixed, they cannot take an early lump sum payout. The monthly amount they will get is set for them as is the amount of survivors' benefits. There are no individual options.

The introduction of DC systems has upset this tidy landscape. There are options to be taken or refused. Workers are now exposed to pension risk without being aware of this. Mere information handed down to them without appropriate literacy is useless and might even prove damaging. Advice might prove not to be impartial or might not be trusted, especially if the memory of past financial crises still lingers. I had a personal experience of this when assessing the Russian pension system in 2002: memory of the financial crisis of 1998 was obviously still vivid and people would not trust investment advice. Mistrust of advice is becoming more common in Europe as a result of the financial crisis whose costs in terms of recession and unemployment are making people look with skepticism even at financial education programs because everything that is "financial" in this particular period is not popular at all.

Dr. Adele Atkinson: I just wanted to also remind everybody that it is not just about financial education. We do not talk about financial education being able to do everything. It is really important that people are well informed, but it is also really important that they are operating within a robust financial consumer protection framework and that regulation is in place. They also need to understand how and where that framework can protect them and, if there is any financial service or any product that is outside of that framework, they need to understand the difference between those that are safe and those that are less safe. We should not see financial education as being able to or even being the right way to solve all of the problems faced by financial consumers. I think that is really important.

Prudence Angelita A. Kasala, Head of the Financial Consumer Protection Department, Bangko Sentral ng Pilipinas: I was just wondering whether the resource persons could give us their thoughts on the effective strategies they have seen in introducing a voluntary retirement product. It is usually difficult to promote voluntary retirement products because people tend to rely on mandatory or state pensions. So when you are trying to push voluntary retirement products, what strategies, aside from product design, have you seen that have been successful?

Prof. Elsa Fornero: First of all, taxation is a very important incentive. If it is announced that a savings product will be favorably taxed with respect to others, people will generally understand this and appreciate it. This has been used in order to "nudge" people into making "reasonable" investment choices. Then there are older, let us say, provisions that you mentioned. Default options are another example of "nudging."

Dr. Julie Agnew: You can also look at the Swedish experience when they rolled out their plan. They ran a big information campaign where lots of people were made aware of the plan features, and from what I understand in the first two years, I might have this wrong, there were fewer people choosing the default, but as soon as that information campaign declined, there were more people defaulting. So providing good information is something that actually cannot be there just at the start-up; there has to be this constant communication with new and existing participants.

Prof. Elsa Fornero: Are you familiar with the letter that the Swedish pension institutions regularly send out to all employed workers? It is called the "orange letter" and it is very, very important because it informs each individual worker of her or his pension situation at that moment. Research discovered that workers are very keen on receiving their own orange letter, and they unreservedly trust its figures. Maybe receiving an actual letter, with an actual (orange) envelope rather than a less distinctive digital communication, has added to its importance. This has resulted in absolute trust in the pension agency and the orange letter is generally kept among important family documents, something to be depended upon and implicitly trusted. The Swedish procedure is almost unique and I can assure you, from my direct experience, that in many countries politicians do not like people being informed in a detailed way about the amount of their future pensions, particularly when a reform has just been enacted or is about to be introduced, that will reduce this amount. Politicians generally prefer, so to speak, to nicely wrap reforms in a nice package, so that they can tell people, "Okay, we have reformed your pension, but we have not 'cut' your pension," which is not really true.

Flore-Anne Messy, Deputy Head, Financial Affairs Division, OECD: Thank you. Yes, the orange envelope, I think, is an interesting example, although a lot of people were not even aware they were receiving the envelope or, as you said, were receiving it and quietly putting it in a drawer and not looking at it. They also surveyed whether people were understanding the content and quite often they did not understand it, which raises the issue about how to inform people about pensions, about risk, and uncertainty. But this is not my question.

My question is more about what you were just saying. I believe in a lot of countries there is a tension between the necessity for transparency about reform in particular and the fact that, indeed, politicians are not very keen on informing. I have been traveling in countries like Spain, for example, where they have just enacted a reform but nobody wants to inform people and the only ones willing to do so are banks, the investment funds. Of course, then the consumers are receiving multiple messages from all these institutions with absolutely no message from the government. So how do we deal with this trade-off, with this tension between the necessity for people to understand the reform and, on the other side, the reluctance to communicate about it? I am not sure you have the solution, but do you have any indication how to gently push people to make them understand? It is very important to inform in a transparent way, otherwise people will be in a worse situation in the future.

Prof. Elsa Fornero: One short remark on this: this was exactly my experience when I was Italian Minister of Labor, in 2011–2013 and was in charge of the pension and labor market reforms. I was acutely aware of the problem of communicating with people, of talking to people. But I was not a political minister, I was a so-called "technocratic minister"; the two main political parties, although providing bipartisan support to the reform in Parliament, were reluctant to convey the message that they considered unpopular. The main message of any such reform has indeed its hard bits, i.e., that you are introducing the reform for the younger generations and that you ask the elder generations to pay a large part of the cost. It however also has a positive core, i.e., the rebalancing of generations, something good to show when you are asking people for sacrifices. But politicians must themselves be convinced and have the stamina. In my case, neither of these conditions applied. So my conclusion is that you need communicators as well as communication.

Ms. Anna Zelentsova: Can I add just a few words on Ms. Messy's question? Yes, I think it is really important and in our case what is good is that we have a mandate for a national financial education project and in this case we are a little bit separate from other parts of the ministry of finance, for financial policy, even it is not within the financial policy department or not under the deputy minister who is responsible for it. So we have a little bit more opportunity to, say, communicate to people.

Prof. Elsa Fornero: Do you mean to say that you are something like an independent authority?

Ms. Anna Zelentsova: Yes, Our position is always that it is better if we communicate it ourselves than if somebody else would say it because when media or other people would criticize reform, they would say it anyway but in a more negative way. So I do not know why other government or political actors do not understand this communication rule—that it is better that we communicate, that it is easier to say clearly what you think is important to say. So we try to do it, to the extent we can.

Sue Lewis, Chair, UK Financial Services Consumer Panel: Just an observation on tax incentives, which I just do not believe work. They are highly regressive and all the evidence shows that they do not generate new savings, only huge dead weight costs. But my final question is actually, is a pension a sensible thing to be doing in an age where people maybe work for 40 years and then live for another 30? I mean, should we not be looking at new products and new ways of managing the lifetime income rather than a pension? I know we can discuss that forever.

Prof. Elsa Fornero: This is a short question, but the answer could indeed be very long. Let me attempt to give some bullet points. First, there is a lot of controversy on taxation and its effects that we certainly cannot introduce here. Second, while I believe pensions will always be necessary, this does not mean that we do not have to look at other products as well: one example stems from the observation that in many countries people own their homes and they could, if they wanted to (it might not be very popular) and the market provided the right instruments, transform it into a lump sum of money, or, more conveniently in a succession of additional monthly payment. Of course there are many, many more possibilities.

But, well, pensions are an insurance against the longevity risk and I really believe that longevity risk is something that people want to be insured against. This can be done, and complemented, in several ways, but I do believe that we will, for the foreseeable future, have pensions and pension problems will be at the center of the stage.

I think we have to stop here. I believe this has been a very interesting session, but I am sure the next one will be very stimulating. Thank you very much.

Target Audiences for Effective Financial Education

Flore-Anne Messy, Deputy Head, Financial Affairs Division, OECD and Executive Secretary of the OECD/International Network on Financial Education (INFE): As you can see, this is the largest panel of the day, so I will be very quick in my moderation. This last session of the day is about target audiences for effective financial education.

Before giving the floor to the panelists, I would like to tell you in two words "why target audiences." Basically we were interested within the OECD and the International Network on Financial Education (INFE) in target audiences because of the results of surveys of financial literacy, which clearly showed that target groups—women, young people, elderly people, migrants, and migrant entrepreneurs—have different levels of financial literacy. Some groups have lower levels of financial literacy, some groups, I would say, have different needs for financial literacy. So if you take women, for example, it seems that they have a low level of financial knowledge and confidence, but they are very good at day-to-day planning. Young people seem to display a lower level of financial literacy on the whole and have difficulty in planning ahead. So there are different reasons, different levels of financial literacy, and different levels of competency.

The second reason is that these different audiences like to learn, like to get information in different ways. Young people may prefer a more interactive way using modern technology in many countries, elderly people tend to favor face-to-face contact and they like to have papers and information that they can keep—so different ways of learning. This is why we really want to spend a moment to look at this for target audiences and look at how different countries are trying to face these needs and also to address their preference for learning.

So with no further ado, I would like to present this impressive panel. We will start with some presentations on Japan, with Ms. Ryoko Okazaki, Director, Head of Promotion of Financial Education Group, Public Relations Department at the Bank of Japan. We will then have Prof. Naoyuki Yoshino, Dean of ADBI, and Prof. Nobuyoshi Yamori, Professor, Research Institute for Economics and Business Administration at Kobe University. They will concentrate on financial education in Japanese secondary schools and high schools.

We will then have a presentation from Prof. Katsuyasu Suzuki, President, Japan Institute of Life Insurance and Professor, Faculty of Law, Teikyo University, and from Mr. Kazumasa Fukada, Managing Director, General Insurance Association of Japan. They will focus on youth and in particular on college students and younger employees. Last but not least, Mr. Hiroshi Ohata, Director for Policy Planning and Research, Policy and Legal Division, Planning and Coordination Bureau at the Financial Services Agency (FSA) of Japan. He will particularly focus on the elderly.

Then we will cross an ocean and we will go to Australia with Mr. Miles Larbey, Head of Financial Education at the Australian Securities and Investments Commission (ASIC). He will partly focus on the case of women. Then we will cross another ocean and go to the Russian Federation and Ms. Anna Zelentsova, Head of Financial Literacy at the Ministry of Finance and Co-chair of the GPFI subgroup on financial consumer protection and financial literacy, who will be the commentator for the session.

So thank you all and with no further ado, I would like to give the floor to Ms. Okazaki.

Overview of Financial Education in Japan

Ryoko Okazaki, Director, Head of Promotion of Financial Education Group, Public Relations Department, Bank of Japan: Ladies and gentlemen, good afternoon. It is a great honor to have a chance to give an overview of financial education in Japan. I thank all of you for coming to exchange ideas and seek better ways. Today, as one of such examples, I would like to explain the activities of the Central and Local Councils for Financial Services Information, of which the Bank of Japan occupies a member seat and also plays the role of the secretariat.

In Japan, financial education dates back to the period right after World War II (Table 3.1), although it started to explicitly aim at the overall improvement of financial literacy only around 2000. The Japanese economy suffered from high inflation and shortage of capital right after the end of World War II and in order to tackle the serious problems savings were promoted.

In the beginning, the government took the lead in promoting savings. However, since the lead taken by the government in promoting savings could easily give the impression that the government was forcing people to save and supporting financial institutions by doing so, instead, the system of local councils for savings promotion, which was voluntarily established by the central bank, financial organizations, economic and industry organizations, women's organizations, and various stakeholders, took the lead of the movement. The Central Council for Savings Promotion, which is the predecessor of the Central Council for Financial Services Information, was established as the central organization for these local councils.

Table 3.1   Savings promotion movements

Year	Savings Promotion
1946	"Savings Campaign for Economic Salvation" was launched, managed mainly by the Ministry of Finance and Bank of Japan, to curb post-war inflation.
1950	Local Council for Savings Promotion started to be established.
1952	The Central Council for Savings Promotion was established.
1958	Savings Practicing Districts were established.
1960	Savings Promoters were appointed.
1973	The system of Schools for Pecuniary Education was introduced, based on the children's bank activities.

Source: Central Council for Financial Services Information (2002).

In this period, grassroots movement occurred, such as encouraging people to manage their households appropriately by disseminating household account books for free, designating model districts in various areas across the country to support savings by various local groups in those districts, and assigning savings promoters to guide such activities of local groups. Children's bank activities for encouraging pupils to save expanded, where pupils deposited their own money while they dealt with clerical works of the banks themselves.

During the high economic growth era, the savings promotion movement changed gradually, shifting from savings promotion to the promotion of life planning and the dissemination of financial and economic knowledge. Then around 2000, more drastic change occurred.

Financial liberalization, which started in Japan in 1970, developed drastically in the 2000s. This process is called the Japanese Financial Big Bang and a "payoff" scheme was restarted in 2005 (Table 3.2). Thanks to dynamic financial liberalization, individuals became capable of choosing and using various financial products and services, which made it necessary for them to choose financial products and services, understanding accompanying risks, and to be responsible for the results of their own choice. Individuals were expected to become independent and to be able to judge financial matters appropriately. Thus, promotion of financial education to improve the ability of consumers to choose and judge—in other words, to improve the financial literacy of consumers—became an urgent issue.

In this movement, the Central Council for Financial Services Information (CCFSI) has been providing various information on the contents of financial products, deposit insurance, and skills related to life planning and contracts, which are necessary to make proper judgments and choices, by organizing a series of lectures throughout the country, developing pamphlets, and enriching the contents of its website. Concerning financial education in schools, the CCFSI named fiscal year 2005 the "First Year of Financial Education" and developed and published its "Financial Education Program" in 2007, aimed at cultivating the zest for life of children, that is, their ability to deal with things independently in society. The program shows the "Contents of Financial Education by Age Groups" and good teaching practices as

Table 3.2 Financial education after financial liberalization
(around 2000 and after)

Year	Financial Education
2001	Central Council for Savings Promotion was renamed Central Council for Financial Services Information and Local Councils for Savings Promotion were renamed Prefectural Councils for Financial Services Information.
2002	Districts for Promotion of Savings and Life Planning were renamed Financial Study Groups, and Promoters of Savings and Life Planning were renamed Financial Services Information Advisers.
2005	The Central Council regarded this fiscal year as the first year of promoting financial education.
2007	The Central Council published the "Financial Education Program."

Notes: As a result of the Japanese Financial Big Bang, individuals were expected to become independent and to be able to judge financial matters appropriately.
Source: Central Council for Financial Services Information website (http://www.shiruporuto.jp/about/us/enkaku/).

well. It has been widely used by teachers in the classroom. The CCFSI has also been organizing seminars for teachers and supporting schools, which study and conduct financial education.

The economic downturn was precipitated by the Lehman Brothers bankruptcy in 2008 as excessive risk taking by individuals was one of the reasons for the international financial crisis, and the importance of financial literacy for the stability of financial markets was recognized internationally. The Financial Services Agency of Japan produced a report on the promotion of financial education in 2013. This report emphasized the behavioral aspects of financial literacy and suggested to focus on the minimum level of financial literacy to be attained by people 20 years old and over. This suggestion deserves special mention in assessing the effectiveness of financial education. The CCFSI, based on this report, is trying to develop detailed content of financial literacy to be attained by age groups, especially adults, as well as preparing to promote financial education more effectively.

We reviewed the transition of financial education in Japan over the past 70 years. Even though there have been changes in emphasis and the methods to promote financial education over the course of time, it seems that the history of financial education has implication for how we think about financial education in future. First, I would like to emphasize that it is very important to secure neutrality and fairness in promoting financial education. The fact that the savings promotion movement, after World War II, was led by the CCFSI and the Local Councils for Financial Services Information, which were set up as voluntary movements, reflects the importance of neutrality and fairness.

However, it is true that tendencies still exist among teachers in the classroom to avoid introducing financial education into their teaching practices. It might be related to the misunderstanding that financial education includes an intention of influencing the choice of financial products by individuals. Therefore, in Japan we developed and shared criteria for neutrality and fairness among financial organizations to promote financial education. Any of us who promote financial education should behave rigorously, securing neutrality and fairness in order to avoid suspicion in this respect.

Next, I would like to emphasize the importance of life planning and household management. Life planning and household management are the most important premises to take appropriate financial action and have been emphasized through both savings promotion activities and current financial education. In the post World War II savings promotion movement, encouragement of the use of household account books was extremely effective in promoting thriftiness and savings among people. In modern life, increasing variety of lifestyles and a sense of value of people made it more important than before for people to be skillful in household management and life planning and think independently.

The great challenge in the promotion of financial education is to make indifferent people interested in financial literacy. It seems to be most effective to show the risk related to one's own life planning to get anyone to recognize the necessity of financial literacy. Thus, it is one of our tasks to provide information on these kinds of risks to people in an easy-to-understand and familiar way.

As I mentioned before, improvement in behavior such as making it a habit to manage households soundly or choosing financial products appropriately is emphasized in Japan, too. In financial education in schools, revision of the "Financial Education Program" is currently underway, putting more emphasis on interest, willingness, and positive attitude toward the content to be learned. However, it takes time to improve people's financial behavior through education. Thinking of good educational ways to control people's potential mental bias, such as deliberate procrastination, could be necessary. In this respect, we consider that knowledge from behavioral economics and consumer psychology might be useful and we would like to keep on learning from these fields.

Lastly, I would like to re-emphasize the importance of financial education in schools. It is by no means unimportant to improve the financial literacy of adults, but I cannot put too much emphasis on the importance of financial education in schools. It is important to start financial education as early as possible and schools are the special place where everyone can learn basically the same content with professionally skilled teachers. Reflecting on the importance of financial education in schools, the CCFSI is trying to revise the Financial Education Program, as I mentioned, right now. It was published in 2007 and the financial literacy map was published last year. We put special emphasis on the revision of the table of contents by age groups. A rich table of contents will be published in the coming months as a result of intensive discussions among relevant stakeholders, including excellent teachers, high-level officers in the Ministry of Education, and experts and representatives from related organizations. After publishing the result of the revision, it will become an effective tool to promote financial education. I believe that the enthusiasm for this revision will give the promotion of financial education as a whole in Japan new momentum. Thank you.

Ms. Flore-Anne Messy: Thank you very much, Ms. Okazaki, for the conference, your overview and for also highlighting a few concepts that are really important. I like the fact that you highlighted neutrality and fairness, which are certainly very important when you consider financial education and how it should be implemented and delivered to consumers. I also liked the fact that you are emphasizing risk and especially risks that are possibly addressed to consumers and individuals and how they perceive the risks and what is the level of risk in their personal lives. So I think it is very important.

Now, I would like to introduce the second presentation, focusing on Japanese secondary and high schools and, of course, financial education.

Financial Education in Japan

Naoyuki Yoshino, Dean, ADBI, and Chief Advisor, FSA Institute: Thank you very much. This paper is jointly written with Prof. Yamori of Kobe University. As is well known, the Asian region is dominated by banks and capital markets are very small. This morning, many people talked about preparation for an aging society and why financial education is important for that. But the study we are presenting looks at secondary schools and high schools, specifically a survey of 4,462 teachers and what is going on in their individual teaching methods and also what kind of problems they are facing. At the same time, many young people use consumer finance and small businesses have difficulty getting loans, and also at the national level in Japan, the government is looking for channels to promote growth and to promote start-up businesses. Those all are purposes of financial education.

First, I would like to talk about this study of junior high school and high school financial education. The results you can get from the website; these are the results obtained in April 2014. The survey is of junior high school and high school teachers. One of the things we found is that financial education is mostly taught in home-making courses and these courses do not specialize in financial education. Many teachers teach home-making, how to cook and so on, and they spend very little time on financial education. The survey was conducted among all junior high schools and high schools and it was sent to 32,220 teachers. We obtained 4,462 responses from teachers and I would like to explain the details of those studies.

Nobuyoshi Yamori, Professor, Research Institute for Economics & Business Administration, Kobe University: My name is Nobuyoshi Yamori, I would like to explain the current situation of financial education in Japanese schools based on the teacher survey that Prof.

Yoshino mentioned. This survey was conducted by a research group chaired by Prof. Yoshino last year. We thank the Japan Securities Dealers Association, which supported this survey research. As far as we know, this is the most comprehensive study on this matter in Japan. Because of time limitations, I will explain it very briefly. If you are interested in the overall results, please visit the website where English as well as Japanese versions are available.

First of all, we asked teachers in charge of financial education about their majors in college. Only 20% of junior high school teachers, for example, graduated from economics departments. The majority of teachers seemed not to have studied much economics when they were university students. Therefore, we recognize that teachers with a lack of financial knowledge are actually in charge of teaching finance in Japan.

This is the answer to the question: what do you think about financial and economic education being taught in schools (Figure 3.1)? Almost all teachers answered "necessary" or "necessary to some extent." Therefore, we can say that teachers commonly agree that financial education in schools is necessary. As the importance of financial education is widely recognized, finance is usually taught in Japanese schools now.

What do you think about financial and economic education being taught in schools?

☐ Necessary ☐ Necessary to some extent ▨ Not really necessary ▪ Unnecessary ▪ No response

	0%	20%	40%	60%	80%	100%

Overall (n=3,128): 37.0 | 58.0 | 4.1 | 0.3 / 0.5

Junior high school (n=2,097): 34.3 | 60.0 | 4.8 | 0.3 / 0.6

High school (n=1,110): 43.2 | 53.3 | 2.8 | 0.3 / 0.4

Reasons Why Financial and Economic Education Is Necessary (%)

	Number of questionnaires	Gain the knowledge required to be a smart consumer	Gain an understanding of the workings of society	Become independent as an individual in the future	Gain a correct sense of the value of money
Overall	4,241	73.5	44.8	38.9	24.6
Junior high school	2,909	77.2	43.7	36.2	24.6
High school	1,436	65.7	47.8	44.6	23.7

Figure 3.1 Teachers agree on necessity of financial and economic education

Source: Study Group on the Promotion of Financial and Economic Education (2014).

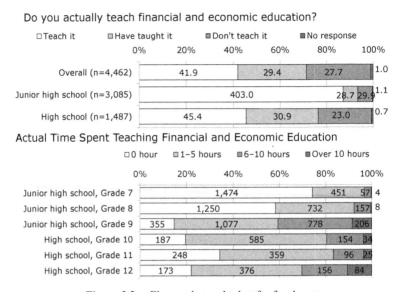

Figure 3.2 Finance is taught, but for few hours

Source: Study Group on the Promotion of Financial and Economic Education (2014).

Although 70% of respondents have teaching experience, teaching time is very limited, that is, it is very rare that finance is taught more than five hours per year (Figure 3.2). Of course, most teachers think that current teaching hours are not enough. The main reason is believed to be that there is no room in the current education program. More than 80% of teachers chose this answer.

In Japan, the Ministry of Education formulates the nationwide education program. Therefore, teachers have very limited power to choose subjects to teach. To increase teaching hours, it is crucial to demand the Ministry of Education to revise an education plan and expand the contents on financial education.

Responding to our question, teachers specify various difficulties in teaching finance. For example, consistent with their academic background, half of the teachers mention lack of expertise among the teachers and the difficulties of teaching finance in schools. This is a detail of the previous sheet. We skip this sheet due to time limitations. However, I would like to add that this regression result suggests that when teachers are not interested in finance, this negatively affects the probability that they actually teach finance. The better the teachers know finance, the more likely they are to teach it.

Using the logistic regression model, we investigate who thinks that the lack of expertise among the teachers is one of the difficulties for teaching finance in schools. Among others, we find that variables representing majors in college are significant, suggesting that teachers' majors in college significantly affect the recognition of the lack of expertise. In other words, many teachers who graduated from departments other than economics feel that they do not have sufficient expertise. We need to support them in order to encourage them to teach finance in schools.

We omit to explain this sheet, but I can mention that a similar implication is obtained by another regression analysis. Here, I summarize our survey as shown. Also, I provide several other results, but I cannot explain them because of the time limitations (Table 3.3).

Table 3.3 What kinds of problems do you see with the study content of current financial and economic education lessons?

	Overall	By school type	
		Junior high school	High school
Number of questionnaires	3,128	2,097	1,110
Focus on understanding terminology or systems makes it difficult for students to relate lessons to their actual lives	55.0	55.6	53.7
Students learn the information, but find it difficult to pick up abilities or attitudes	40.9	42.1	37.4
Financial and economic education is relegated to specific grades and timeframes, making it impossible to have ongoing studies in the subject	31.6	32.3	30.9
There is little practical knowledge, such as types of interest rates or financial products and the relationship between risk and return	28.3	24.7	35.0
Difficult for students to gain any basic skills needed to be independent, such as managing income and expenses and savings	22.2	20.7	24.8
Do not see any particular problems	5.5	6.0	4.1
Others	3.1	2.7	3.8
No response	2.3	2.3	2.3

Source: Study Group on the Promotion of Financial and Economic Education (2014).

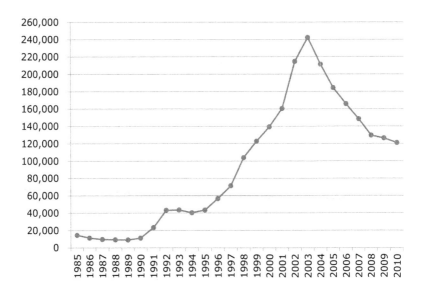

Figure 3.3   Number of households' default

Source: Ministry of Justice.

Dean Naoyuki Yoshino: Thank you. If we look at the last page, this is a typical answer of the teachers. Many students think this topic is very difficult and also the teachers do not have so much knowledge about these subjects. Those are the major problems we are facing in Japan. So now we are trying to make a kind of textbook for junior schools and high schools and we will also provide video lectures for those teachers. I found that teachers prefer to give about half of the lectures by themselves, so in other words, if there are 40 minutes of lecture, then 20 minutes would be video, and then for 20 minutes the teachers will use their own materials, and so on. There are 15 weeks in the Japanese curriculum so that we are now planning to make textbooks for high school and junior high school students. I am teaching at Open University by television every week, for 15 weeks, which will be shown every week on Japanese TV. We are presenting those subjects by this method.

I think the purpose of financial education is to teach about consumer finance and consumer credit. Figure 3.3 shows the number of defaults of Japanese households. You can see that the peak was around 2002–2003 and

1. Bank Loans – relatively safe borrowers
2. Hometown Investment Trust Funds – SME

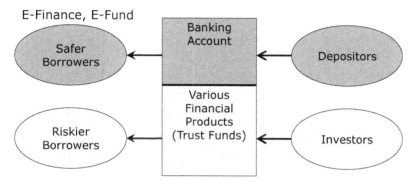

Figure 3.4   Start-up businesses and SME financing by hometown investment trust funds

Note: SMEs = small and medium-sized enterprises.
Source: Author.

then it started to decline. This is mainly due to the fact that we have set an interest rate ceiling for money lenders, and we have also started consumer financial education for individuals. Another target of financial education is small and medium-sized enterprises (SMEs). We have started to collect data for an SME database of those firms that are borrowing from banks. A total of 14.4 million data points were collected from SMEs. During this process, SME owners have to keep their books and keep track of their revenues and expenses, which became a very good financial education for them. So not only consumers, but also business people, have very much benefited from these financial skills. The Asian economy is dominated by SMEs, so this is a very important tool to educate those people.

Last is a new method to provide risk capital to help create start-up businesses. Asia is dominated by the banking sector and the Basel capital requirements will restrict the amount of loans from the banking sector. Japan and some Asian countries, Cambodia and Viet Nam, and Peru in South America started what we call hometown investment trust funds (Figure 3.4). These would be provided to start-up businesses, farmers, and so on. In order to provide a much wider variety of investment products, people have to study about returns and risks. Then, based on these returns and risks, hopefully Asian capital markets will develop further, and then the hometown investment trust funds, venture business, banking business and capital markets together could create a very wide range of financial products and access to finance. Those are the goals of financial education in Asia. Thank you very much.

Ms. Flore-Anne Messy: Thank you very much, Dean Yoshino and Prof. Yamori. I was very interested in your presentation and especially in the terminology you were using. When we developed our PISA financial literacy assessment, we also had a questionnaire for teachers. It was quite interesting to see that, indeed, the number of hours that teachers are actually teaching financial education is very limited in the countries that participated in the exercise—I think it was less than two hours per year, so very little.

What is interesting for me is that in your questionnaire you are speaking not only about financial education, but also about economic education; I will have some questions about how you manage with such a wide scope of issue potentially.

Now I would like to give the floor to our second duo of speakers. Please come to the podium, Prof. Suzuki and Mr. Fukada. Their presentation will focus on college students and younger employees.

Financial Education Aimed at the Youth (College Students and Younger Employees) in Japan

Katsuyasu Suzuki, President, Japan Institute of Life Insurance; and Professor, Faculty of Law, Teikyo University: Yes, thanks so much for your introduction, Madam Moderator. Good afternoon, ladies and gentlemen. I am Katsuyasu Suzuki from the Japan Institute of Life Insurance (JILI). Today I would like to briefly explain some of our most important activities of financial education aimed at college students and younger employees.

Before starting with the explanation of Figure 3.5, some information of JILI's activities. We have been providing a wide range of people, including consumers and the youth, with information related to life

Major Means of Life Protection

There are three pillars of life protection: **social security** as a national welfare policy, **job-based coverage** as a welfare program for employees, and **private coverage** prepared, respectively.

	Social Security	Job-based Coverage	Private Coverage
Death →	Survivors' basic pension, survivors' welfare pension	Preretirement death benefit, solatium, survivors' pension	Term life insurance, whole life insurance
Injury or sickness →	Health insurance, disability basic pension, disability employees' pension	Workers' accident compensation insurance	Medical insurance, accident insurance, savings
Old age →	Old-age basic pension, old-age employees' pension	Retirement allowance, company pension	Personal pension, savings
Nursing care →	Nursing care insurance	Family care leave	Nursing care insurance, savings
Residential fire Natural disaster →	Solatia for disaster, disaster loan	Special payment for disaster	Fire insurance, earthquake insurance
Liability for damages →			Compulsory automobile liability insurance, liability insurance, automobile insurance, insurance for all sorts of recreational activities
Others →			Collision insurance, insurance for all sorts of recreational activities
	* Social security includes national and prefectural government coverage.	* Job-based coverage varies according to companies.	* There are other private coverage types, such as mutual insurance in addition to the examples issued above

Figure 3.5   When and how: needs and means of life protection

Source: Japan Institute of Life Insurance.

planning and life insurance options from a neutral standpoint for almost 40 years to support the enhancement of people's lives by the sound development of the insurance system.

Now let me start with the first activity—a practical learning course for college students. This is surely the core of our financial education for our college students. In the course, our staffers conduct a course for 60 or 90 minutes when requested by teachers or professors to utilize some of their classroom time. The course is held mainly at colleges, sometimes at high schools as well, and is designed for students to learn basic knowledge of life planning and life insurance. In the reference paper entitled "Living and Risk Management," you can find a partial excerpt from our original text used in the course.

There are three key points in the course. Firstly, the importance of life protection in life planning. Secondly, the roles of insurance in life protection. And lastly, the characteristics of procedures relating to insurance contracts. The paper also shows expectations for education at college students mentioned in the Act on Promotion of Consumer

Education (the Act) and in the Financial Literacy Map. I am sure our practical learning course will meet those expectations.

Starting from 1981, the number of times it was held and the numbers of participants in the course shows steady growth, even some exponential growth recently, in the last three years (Figure 3.6). Please note that the gap between the two columns is whether it contains high schools or not. The number of requests from high schools, especially from home-economics teachers, has been increasing recently. I believe this trend might reflect how deeply people felt the need for life protection, especially after the occurrence of the Great East Japan Earthquake and tsunami in 2011.

Of course, the recent discussion on the promotion of consumer education and the Act (2012) should have contributed a lot to it, and our advertising of the activities of this practical learning course, which has been built up quietly over 30 years of experience, came to be gradually but widely accepted by the field of education.

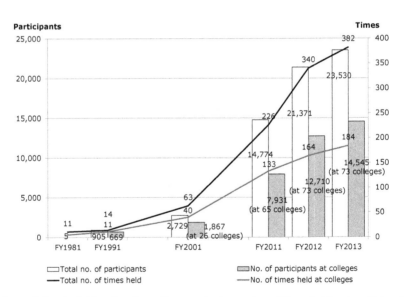

Figure 3.6   Activities aimed at college students: number of times held and participants of the course

Source: Japan Institute of Life Insurance.

The next activity I am introducing is aimed at younger employees. We provide them with basic knowledge of life insurance they need when they face important life stages. More specifically, we hand out a brochure entitled "The ABCs of Insurance for Beginners" free of charge (Figure 3.7). We do so at the graduation ceremony of vocational high schools, which is right before the life stage of starting to work, and at the annual coming-of-age ceremony, which is right before officially becoming an adult, and, with the cooperation of the Board of Education, at childbirth classes and health centers, which is right before starting to raise a child. We distributed more than 270,000 copies last fiscal year.

Now please let me move on to the last one—our new online content entitled e-Life Planning. We at JILI will release the program on our website this March. We are struggling right now to develop it. It is a life planning simulation program, originally developed from the point of view of supporting people in thinking and planning on their own at each life stage. By using this program, people can actually experience to imagine

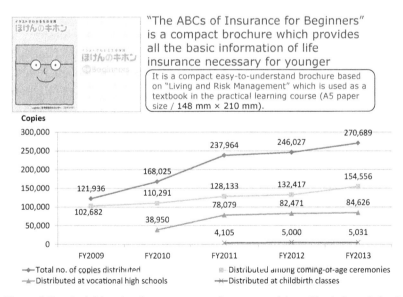

Figure 3.7   Activities aimed at younger employees: provision of basic knowledge by distributing a brochure

Source: Japan Institute of Life Insurance.

their dreams, goals, and to make plans to fulfill them, to grasp the present situation of their household finances, such as how much in assets and liabilities they have, and think about preparations for large outlays in the future, including considering financial risks caused by unexpected accidents at the various key life stages, starting to work, starting to think about marriage, and starting to raise a child.

I believe that making life plans at each life stage repeatedly by using this program should make them realize the importance of life planning and improve their literacy in risk management and insurance. Now, that is all for today. I appreciate today's opportunity and it would be greatly appreciated if my presentation today could be a little useful to you. Thank you very much.

General Insurance Association of Japan (GIAJ) Financial Education Initiatives for the Younger Generation in Japan

Kazumasa Fukada, Managing Director, General Insurance Association of Japan: Good afternoon, ladies and gentlemen. I would like to thank everyone present here today for this opportunity to introduce the activities of the General Insurance Association of Japan (GIAJ). I am Kazumasa Fukada of the GIAJ and I will be making a presentation on financial education for university students and junior corporate citizens in Japan.

Since general insurance is an intangible product, it is important to ensure consumers gain an accurate understanding of its functions. In this respect, insurance companies wholly assume accountability while we are asking consumers to improve their literacy on the subject. For this reason, we at the GIAJ are working to improve general insurance literacy mainly by dispatching lecturers to various institutions and developing educational tools.

Before getting into the main discussion, I would like to give an overview of our existing activities on insurance education. For primary and junior high school students, our safety education program called Disaster Prevention Duck is carried out to help children recognize risks faced every day. Children run facilities in their towns associated with disaster prevention, crime prevention, and traffic safety. Next for high school students, lectures cover financial damage in the event of a realized risk and methods to cope with such events. In addition, supplementary materials are provided to teachers for use in class. Then for university students and junior corporate citizens, details of insurance are explained. Lastly, for general consumers, including the elderly, seminars and educational tools which have been developed and published on the website are provided with the purpose of informing the general public of the requirement amounts and appropriate products.

Now I would like to move on to today's topic. Concrete measures include the free dispatch of lecturers from the GIAJ, the organization of single or a series of seminars at universities nationwide, and development of educational tools for university students and junior corporate citizens. Firstly, most seminars begin with an introduction to general insurance, to educate students about their risks, followed by an overview of general insurance focusing on key areas of protection, including auto insurance and fire insurance, etc. They also provide cautionary advice about purchasing insurance policies. The aim of the seminars is to help university students recognize personal risks and acquire the ability to properly compare and select insurance products that meet their individual needs. At the end of December 2014, 51 seminars had been attended by 6,600 university students.

Next, a series of seminars at universities aim to disseminate factual information on general insurance in a systematic and detailed manner to help students gain an understanding of the needs and roles of general insurance in the national economy. The GIAJ has presented these seminars since 2010. For the faculties of economics and commerce, the contents of the seminars include an overview of key insurance products, risk management, and the general insurance market. For the faculty of law, the topics covered include knowledge on the Insurance Business Act, the Insurance Act, the concept of indemnity, and consumer protection laws. The curriculum is decided upon consultation with the universities in question. In the areas of risk management and risk financing, case studies are introduced to ensure that the contents are relevant to everyday life. During 2014, GIAJ staff organized accredited seminars on general insurance, a total of 15 units which were attended by approximately 1,400 students at 15 universities.

Now I would like to show an example of our educational tools developed for university students and junior corporate citizens—an introductory brochure called Freshers' Guide provided at the seminars. This guide is also on the website of GIAJ for everyone to browse. In the first part of the guide, the causes of accidents and functions and mechanism of insurance are explained in an easy-to-understand quiz format. In the latter half, protection, preparation for risky events, in other words, general insurance, is explained with various scenes familiar to young people, such as overseas travel, owning a car, and single life experiences. Lastly, it shows our planned future initiatives.

These are our main thoughts and activities on financial education for the younger generation in Japan. Thank you for your attention.

Ms. Flore-Anne Messy: Thank you very much, Mr. Fukada. I think it was very interesting also to see that the GIAJ in Japan is very active in trying to develop financial education for young people. It is a good case study that we are showing that the association and the private sector have an important role to play in financial education, especially in complex matters such as insurance. During the Q&A, we would particularly like to discuss with you how you manage to effectively teach this complex concept.

Now we are changing age group, we will deal with the elderly, which we know is a particularly vulnerable group who are most in need of financial education. Mr. Ohata, the floor is yours.

Financial Education for Elderly People in Japan

Hiroshi Ohata, Director for Policy Planning and Research, Policy and Legal Division, Planning and Coordination Bureau, FSA: Thank you very much. Good afternoon, ladies and gentlemen. It is a great honor for me to be giving you this presentation. I am going to talk about financial education for elderly people. First, I will show you the elderly people's mindset and financial assets and then I will explain the FSA's strategy for financial education for the elderly. Okay, let me start by telling you about their mindset.

As you may know, Japan is rapidly aging. The elderly population is growing and the share of the population aged 65 and over is increasing. Currently, it is estimated that this share will reach about 40% in 2060, so the government of Japan is taking measures to solve the problems. Anyway, there are many elderly people and the number is increasing.

Based on such a situation, I will show you their mindset. Living expenses in retirement are the most important purpose of holding financial assets and the most favored financial asset is savings. In addition, the elderly tend to be confident in their own financial literacy. At the same time, they have a tendency to be unwilling to collect information. It should be noted that many elderly people, who have had fewer opportunities for financial education, have ended up in financial trouble and have been scammed, such as through a fraudulent statement like "You will be able to gain high profit without risk."

Next, as for financial assets, they are concentrated among elderly people. They hold about 60% of individual financial assets in Japan. Most of them are savings. At the same time, there is a significant diversity of asset accumulation among the elderly and it should be noted that the amount and composition of financial assets vary in each elderly household. As I mentioned, the elderly hold many assets as a whole and they have more possibilities to suffer from financial trouble. So I would say financial education is also important for the elderly people.

Next, let me explain three approaches of the FSA (Figure 3.8). First, the Integrated Approach. The FSA provides financial education and supervises financial institutions to protect financial consumers. For example, the Financial Literacy Map was developed last year. The map shows the minimum required financial literacy and illustrates educational contents for each age group from elementary school students to the elderly people. Also, in order to prevent financial consumers from getting into trouble, the FSA provides them with advice through its helpline. Furthermore, the FSA supervises financial institutions to prevent trouble, especially in case of soliciting elderly people. It goes like this: the FSA provides financial education and supervises financial institutions in order to protect financial consumers. We are taking such measures in an integrated manner.

Integrated Approach

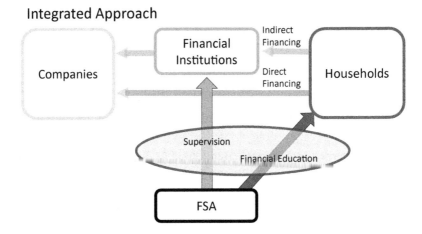

Figure 3.8   FSA's strategy of financial education for the elderly:
Integrated Approach

Source: Financial Services Agency.

Public–Private Coordination Approach

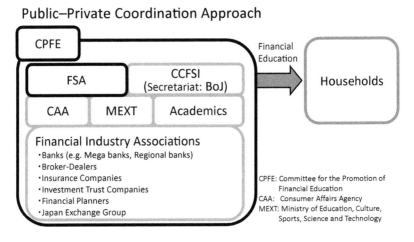

Figure 3.9   FSA's strategy of financial education for the elderly:
Public–Private Coordination Approach

Source: Financial Services Agency.

Community-Based Approach

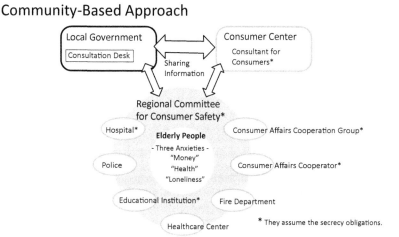

Figure 3.10   FSA's strategy of financial education for the elderly:
Community-Based Approach

Source: Financial Services Agency.

The second approach is the Public–Private Coordination Approach (Figure 3.9). The FSA provides financial education. In addition, we cooperate with CCFSI, Bank of Japan, Ministry of Education, Consumer Affairs Agency, academics, including Prof. Yoshino, ADBI, and financial industry associations. All of them are members of the Committee for the Promotion of Financial Education. We cooperate with each other in providing financial education.

Finally, the Community-Based Approach. The Consumer Safety Act was revised last year. Based on the revision, each local government may establish a Regional Committee for Consumer Safety after the middle of next year in order to prevent consumers from suffering damage. So we are discussing the possibility of using the committee to promote financial education and financial consumer protection.

This is a conceptual chart of the committee, which will cooperate with a local government and a consumer center (Figure 3.10). The Consumer Affairs Agency is now preparing a guideline to operate this system. In this way, we are making great efforts to promote financial education for the elderly through every possible approach. Thank you very much for your attention.

Ms. Flore-Anne Messy: Thank you very much, Mr. Ohata. I think the approach you are taking to facing the needs of the elderly population is very comprehensive, I am impressed by your approach. I think it is also a very interesting case study where financial consumer protection and financial education should indeed really be combined, especially to avoid elderly people facing fraud and abusers and issues like that. I am also interested in your mindset and the mindset that you are presenting at the beginning and especially the fact that the elderly population seems to be quite confident about their financial abilities. I would like to ask you if maybe there is a gender bias here, but we will discuss that after the panel.

Mr. Miles Larbey, can I ask you to present to us the case of women in Australia? Thank you.

Women and Financial Literacy

Miles Larbey, Senior Executive Leader, Financial Literacy, ASIC: Thank you very much and good afternoon again, everybody. I should probably point out that there are many, many capable women in my team back at ASIC who would have been more than happy to come and give this presentation but were not available to do so.

So as I was saying earlier, ASIC is responsible for, among other things, Australia's national financial literacy strategy. We lead and coordinate that strategy which is for many, many different stakeholders. One of the things that that strategy does is identify a number of target audiences and women are one of the target audiences in the strategy. That is partly in response to findings around financial literacy levels, which I will talk about in a bit more detail in a moment, but primarily I think more in response to some structural issues which generally mean that women end up with lower balances in their retirement savings than men and these issues are things such as women tending to spend more time out of the workforce than men, caring for children or elderly parents, women having longer life expectancies than men and women, as I was saying previously in my other presentation, certainly have lower amounts of money accumulated in retirement savings at retirement and also less participation in the retirement savings system altogether. So I suppose this might be an area where through financial literacy we are also trying to pick up on the concept of financial inclusion as well in terms of making women a priority audience in our strategy. That is just a framework of the behaviors that we consider contribute to financial literacy.

The national survey of financial literacy in Australia identifies groups where there may be lower levels of financial literacy and generally women have been among those groups. So as I say, there are some issues around financial literacy, but that is not the only driver. I think it is important, and our strategy specifically sets this out, that financial literacy or financial knowledge, if you like knowledge and skills, is really only ever one driver of a financial decision. In the strategy, we have tried to take account much more than in the previous one of behavioral economics findings and lessons and present a much better understanding that financial decisions are driven by many different influences. I think that is important when you think about some of the situations around, as I say, retirement planning or household budgeting or whatever it might be.

Okay, so at ASIC we have actually been doing some more detailed research recently to try and understand the behaviors and attitudes of Australian consumers and investors in relation to money. This is to supplement our national strategy, which is conducted every three years. This is a much more targeted and succinct piece of work. One of the things it does do is look at differences between the behaviors and attitudes held by men and women. So what we find here is a more complex picture, I think, than just simply saying, well women have lower levels of financial literacy than men and I think that is incredibly important. We found that generally women and men had similar financial attitudes and behaviors, including similar rates of product ownership, apart from credit cards, with men more likely to have credit cards. Women are more likely to say they have saved money in a six-month period, but more likely to have saved money outside of an automatically direct debt linked arrangement.

One thing that is interesting in this is about attitudes (see Box 3.1). Women say they are more likely than men to agree that dealing with money is stressful and they are more likely to say that they have difficulty

Box 3.1   Women's behaviors and attitudes toward money

Risk/return trade-off

Women (23%) are less likely to say they have heard of and understand the concept of risk/return trade-off than men (38%)

Diversification

Women (34%) are less likely to report they have heard of and understand the concept of diversification than men (47%).

Other investments

Women (31%) are less likely than men (41%) to have investments other than their superannuation and/or home.

Losing money

Women (9%) are significantly less likely than men (22%) to say they had lost money.

Source: ASIC.

understanding financial matters. But, in relation to managing finances, while both men and women have similar levels in terms of people who think they are managing major financial issues in the household, men are more likely to believe they are mostly managing major financial issues while women are under the impression they are jointly managing major financial decisions. So there is clearly a mismatch in terms of perhaps overconfidence or self-belief in terms of what you are actually responsible for between men and women, which may explain some of these findings.

Interestingly, women are much more likely than men to be open about discussing finances within the family or with their children and when it comes to investing—I suppose this is where we found the greatest differences between men's and women's understanding of finances— women say they are less likely to understand risk return, less likely to understand diversification, and certainly have less ownership of investments. But then on the flip side of that, women are much less likely than men to have lost money, including money that they cannot afford. So I think it is a more complex picture and one that we need to understand as we develop strategies around financial education targeting women.

Box 3.2 "Building women's economic security and financial wellbeing" project

---

Stage 1 consultation – Stakeholder forum

- Purpose: to gain support and receive feedback on the concept
- Held August 2014, in Sydney
- Community, government, and corporate stakeholders
- Stakeholders overwhelmingly endorsed the project

Stage 2 – Resource development

- A money "toolkit" with tailored and engaging information
- Career break calculator
- Online training module for intermediaries

Stage 2 – Communication strategy

- Embed resources
- Distribute through networks
- Promotional campaign
- Social media

Source: ASIC.

We have also talked to a number of stakeholders from different stakeholder groups who have given us advice about effective ways to reach out to women in terms of financial education strategies. The importance of partnerships really came through—the importance of delivering education at teachable moments and using existing networks and programs wherever possible. In Australia, and I am sure it is the same in Japan and other countries, there are quite a significant number of community groups that have been developed by women's groups and so the important thing is to build on those networks rather than try and reinvent the wheel, I suppose.

So at ASIC, through our MoneySmart program, we have a range of financial literacy resources at the moment which have been developed specifically for women. What we do is try and tailor this material as much as possible, tailor the information to issues that we think are of concern to women. As I said, we have got a lot of stuff around superannuation and retirement saving. We also try and use real life case studies to make the information more engaging. Interestingly, we are doing quite a lot in social media at the moment and we have a growing Facebook community and our Facebook community is about 75% comprised of women, which is very interesting, so we find social media is a good way to distribute messages to women.

Having identified women as a target group in our strategy, we are currently working on a new project (Box 3.2) with the Australian Government's Office for Women to develop a financial economic security and financial wellbeing toolkit if you like. So this is a new project which is currently underway and what we are trying to do is something much more fulsome and accessible than the various bits of webpages and communications I was just describing. So as I say, we are working in partnership with the government's Office for Women. We held a stakeholder forum a couple of months ago with about 40 stakeholders from nongovernment organizations (NGOs), from the corporate sector, from the government, there were academics, representatives from the Girl Guides, all sorts of groups, and what we are doing is we are developing, we are calling it a toolkit at the moment, that is the working title, aimed at people, women in the about 25–45 age bracket. The idea is that if we can help them at that point to make the most of their money, then issues that we see with elderly women not having nearly enough money in retirement, can be addressed before they crystallize.

One of the products we are looking at is, as I said, women are more likely to have broken workforce participation patterns than men, so we are looking at how we can develop a career break calculator which will show people the impact of taking time out of the workforce and also be linked into other sources of advice and information about what services and assistance is available.

There are a number of other programs running in Australia around financial education and, as I said, they all touch on financial inclusion. There are some matched savings programs. I suppose the point of highlighting these is that the participants overwhelmingly tend to be women in these programs. We have a system of no-interest loan schemes in Australia which are exactly what they say, they are administered by community groups, they are alternatives to payday loans which have been a bit of an issue in Australia and I know in other countries as well. Again, overwhelmingly the recipients of these loans are women. That is just another couple of examples.

So to summarize, the research shows that there are a number of issues facing women that are particular to women and different to men. The strategy has identified women as a key target audience and we are working with others in partnership to try and address those needs. Thank you.

Ms. Flore-Anne Messy: Thank you very much, Mr. Larbey, first for not trying to oversimplify the subject. I really like the fact, and we are trying to stress this also within our INFE, that it is not that women have a lower level of financial literacy—there are differences in the financial literacy needs of men and women and it is really important to stress that. For example, women seem to be more risk averse. Well, there are advantages and drawbacks to that particular characteristic and, by the way, not all women are risk averse. So we should not really try to oversimplify and try to understand this target audience. What I also like is that you are trying to build up a comprehensive project that is not only looking at what financial education can do, but really toward the objective of improving wellbeing. One of the other characteristics of women in almost all countries is that, first, they live longer, and second, they will have fewer resources in old age than men. This is something that really needs to be addressed by financial education.

Having said that, I am pleased to give the floor to Anna Zelentsova who is our commentator for this session.

Comments

Anna Zelentsova, Head of Financial Literacy at Ministry of Finance, co-chair of the Global Partnership on Financial Inclusion: Thank you very much, Ms. Messy. Actually thank you for your help, you already commented and gave very valuable comments, and thank you very much to the speakers. I think it was a really interesting and brilliant presentation of different cases. We see here the Japanese case and the Australian case, and although we do not have financial education rankings of countries, we do know that both of these countries have a rich and long-term experience in financial education. They have already taken a few steps, they already revised their financial literacy strategy or financial education programs. So I think we all have a lot to learn from this experience.

What I put in my list after the presentation is lessons but also challenges, which I think we all face. Some of the challenges are really universal. We discuss them in the Russian Federation, we discuss them at the OECD in their meetings, such as first of all information. We have a dilemma—we need to provide information for consumers, for people, but it should not be too much information because then it can be even more problematic for people to understand and they will lose their interest in financial information. So it is important not to provide too much information, and information that is not too complicated, is neutral, and is fair. For example, in the Russian Federation we now try to test all information we use in our projects with focus groups first. So before we pilot, even before we go to consumers, first we do a focus group and just check if people understand the information we provided. I think it was an important lesson.

Second, financial education in schools, of course, is a huge topic, and a very important direction of financial education. All of our countries are members of the Asia-Pacific Economic Cooperation (APEC) forum and I would just like to remind you that in 2012 the finance ministers of APEC economies made a special joint statement on the importance of financial education in schools. So I think that in this region there is a lot of experience in financial education, but there are also a lot of challenges. First of all, curriculum. We all speak about curriculum and that it is overcrowded, too many subjects, parents worry about it, teachers worry about it, children do not want more subjects, so how to deal with it? There are different examples. Mr. Larbey did not give this example today as he spoke about women, but Australia integrates financial literacy into other obligatory subjects. Japan has their own programs, for example. Different countries have different strategies, but we all need to think how to deal with financial education for young people.

But second are teachers. It is an advantage and disadvantage. If we advocate and lobby for financial education in schools, who will teach those subjects? Because teachers lack expertise and in many cases students do not trust, do not respect them as financial experts, as they are not usually rich people. They are not very financially literate. What to do about this situation, how to train them, how to provide ongoing support for teachers? Is there a role for the private sector here, as Ms. Messy already mentioned in her question? If there is a role, again, how to be neutral? The OECD developed the principles for participation of the private sector in financial education programs. I think it is very important.

We had a very good example of insurance education from Japan, which organizes its own program, a wide program, not marketing, but a real financial education program. I think it is very important to launch such cases, such examples. Then what else? The quality of materials of course. Here, again, the role of regulators and probably private sectors is important, because teachers or educators cannot write materials with good quality by themselves; we need experts there. Using consumer psychology. I personally like this topic very much and I think that it is very important to use a positive attitude approach. But on the other hand, there is the dilemma how to talk about it, how to speak about risks while not being too negative. Because people can become afraid when we talk about all the risks and may not want to invest at all as they think there are too many risks. So the question is, how to find the right balance between a positive attitude and explaining all the risks?

Another important thing that Mr. Larbey mentioned about real life examples, social media, using it for women. I think it is really important to learn about the profiles of target audiences, which all examples were about, to learn about profiles and understand their stronger sides and their advantages and disadvantages, as Ms. Messy also mentioned. We should not just blame women for being less financially literate for example, but learn how to reach them, how to use their strong points, and also how to fill the gaps in their financial knowledge or qualities. This is not only relevant to women. I think it applies to all target audiences, that we need to better understand them.

From this point of view, I also have a question which we tried to solve in the Russian Federation, and I know that internationally it is also important—how to reach those who are most in need? Because in many cases, people who already understand that they need financial knowledge, they can find information; we provide information, we all put a lot of effort into this. But those who do not understand that they need such knowledge, such information—how to reach them, how to explain it to them, how to convince them that they need that? I think that is very important.

Of course a very interesting and important case is that of elderly people. I think the importance of the elderly is still less recognized internationally. Of course, the OECD does a lot in this area already, but in the G20 and in APEC, we talked a lot about women, about young people, about migrants, but less about the elderly. Especially as there is a growing elderly population, it is important to focus on it and to look at specific financial products and financial education, as mentioned already by others earlier in the session. It is really important to look at it from a different, from an alternative point of view. So these are my comments and I do not know, Ms. Messy, if you want to give people a chance to ask questions.

Ms. Flore-Anne Messy: Yes, I am going to give you the chance to ask questions. I would just like react to your point on elderly people. It is true that at the international level there has not been much work on the elderly. I have to say that countries like the United States or Canada specifically told us that this is one of their priorities and they are really trying to develop financial education for elderly people. It is also the case in countries like Japan and Singapore. So clearly, there is an emerging trend and this is certainly something that we will want to address at the OECD.

I would like to add that in the case of elderly people, it is really important to also emphasize the need for financial consumer protection because one of the major issues is that they are often victims of fraud, especially elderly males are often victims of fraud in many countries. So this is certainly something that we have to look at more specifically. Please, I know you have a specific question for us.

Ms. Anna Zelentsova: Yes, thank you very much. Yes, I have a question. My first question is to Ms. Ryoko Okazaki. You mentioned this new financial education or revised financial education program and that you use more behavioral economics or behavioral finance findings for that. Can you give any examples how it would change the program or approaches or target audiences in your financial education program?

Ms. Ryoko Okazaki: I mentioned behavioral economics and consumer psychology and financial education program, but we have not incorporated those in our Financial Education Program, which is one of our national strategies for financial education. However, we have introduced behavioral economics and consumer psychology in several actual financial education programs, such as seminars for teachers and educational events for kids and parents. For example, in our seminars for teachers, we invited a famous professor in the field of behavioral economics who gave a lecture and he provided tips for teachers to increase the attractiveness of their teaching of economic matters and financial matters giving them good examples from behavioral economics concerning people's tendency to procrastinate.

We also had a chance to include consumer psychology in some talk sessions for children and parents. Our lecturer told them some stories about the behavior of shopkeepers utilizing consumer psychology, which they enjoyed and they learned a lot about how to spend money wisely. So those are examples, but we are still learning more about behavioral economics and consumer psychology and I would like to do more to use insights from those fields.

Ms. Anna Zelentsova: Thank you. Thank you very much. Next question to Dean Naoyuki Yoshino and Prof. Nobuyoshi Yamori. You told us about issues of financial education in schools and mentioned that teachers are critically important. What is most important, what kind of support do you think is most important for teachers? By whom and how can this support be provided and is there any role for parents in financial education in schools?

Dean Naoyuki Yoshino: I think in the presentation the point was made that some teachers do not have any basic background in economics and they are very specialized in home economics and so on. How to educate those teachers would be very important. So education methods will be undergoing changes. Secondly, some of the classes would preferably be taught by video or other people, and providing lectures by specialists will be very important. Teachers would then add their own explanations. Also, as part of our study, we gave some example lectures in several high schools, to see how much students will understand the contents. So we are now planning to make some good textbooks for high school and junior high school students.

Prof. Nobuyoshi Yamori: I would like to add something. Actually in our survey, we ask teachers what type of support they would like to have in teaching finance and economic education. Over 70% of teachers answered they would like to have simple supplementary materials that are easy for students to use. The next most desirable support was training seminars where teachers can get financial and economic expertise, which is consistent with our finding that many teachers feel they have a lack of financial expertise.

Also, 25% of teachers replied they would like to see outside lecturers dispatched to their schools. As Prof. Suzuki and Mr. Fukada explained, Japan's financial industry may actually contribute to financial education by providing easy-to-use materials and send their financial experts to schools to give lectures.

Dean Naoyuki Yoshino: One point regarding your comment on neutral information—I think the central bank and government Financial Services Agency can provide neutral information. Sometimes financial industry organizations in the first instance provide neutral information, but then they try to explain their own products. So I think there are some neutrality issues associated with this.

Ms. Anna Zelentsova: No, that was my point. Yes.

Dean Naoyuki Yoshino: Some of the companies maybe.

Ms. Flore-Anne Messy: This is why at the OECD we really promote the role of the associations versus particular companies.

Dean Naoyuki Yoshino: That is a kind of social activity, yes.

Ms. Flore-Anne Messy: The social responsibility, yes, of the association. Just a quick question for you two on training teachers. I know that some countries are developing e-learning and simulated learning, so I was wondering whether you see a place for internet platforms for learning for teachers on this particular topic.

Dean Naoyuki Yoshino: We are now definitely planning to create such video programs, so teachers can take those video lessons any time they want. We are planning to distribute those CD products to the teachers.

Ms. Flore-Anne Messy: Do you have any helpline, because I was always wondering, about this e-learning, maybe teachers have questions. I mean this is not something they are confident about, so do you also have a kind of helpline?

Dean Naoyuki Yoshino: Probably in future, if the money is provided from somewhere, I am sure we can provide those facilities too.

Ms. Anna Zelentsova: Thank you. I can say that we are now developing online learning, but we also learned from our surveys that teachers also like to meet with each other and some of them are quite conservative and use the Internet less. So I think it depends also on culture, on what country. So it is good to use both offline and online tools.

Thank you very much again and my next question, Prof. Katsuyasu Suzuki, goes to you and Mr. Kazumasa Fukada. You provide financial education to young people on such, as Ms. Messy already said, complex issues, complex concepts. Especially as young people do not want to think about risks and problems, how can you reach them, how can you motivate them? Especially from the point of view of the association, how do you convince your colleagues, your members to do these things in a socially responsible way?

Prof. Katsuyasu Suzuki: Thank you very much. It is a very good question and an important question. First, we use a lot of illustrations that are I think the result of our experience. Sometimes, we have had the study group consulting with the honorable scholars and professors. Today I believe that there are some here, including Prof. Nishimura and Prof. Yamori, and on the basis of those results, we are making our textbooks easy to learn from. Diagrams are especially important in the textbook to make it easier to understand. A specific example would be how much it costs in the case of an accident or a sickness, so that young people can imagine realistically. We ask that they completely explain the case in question to the young people and conduct the course, ask many questions in order to make students proactive. I think it is not a good way to just provide lectures because, I think it is important to understand some specific accidents to produce specific questions and answers.

Second, to approach younger employees, we distributed brochures, as I mentioned in my presentation, at the coming-of-age ceremonies, vocational high schools, and childbirth classes. In my personal view, nowadays young people are getting more concerned about these matters. I would like to point out that our courses are not compulsory. I think it is very, very spontaneous, they would desire to have the knowledge. Courses are conducted at the request of schools or companies and the scholars and professors at college or universities. The number of requests is increasing as a result of our steady promotional activities such as direct mail advertising and word-of-mouth advertising. That is very good and important I think. More and more young people are now interested in these matters, and also I think the scholars.

I think that a useful way to promote financial literacy is to strengthen that network between us and the academic associations, the scholars, and professors. We would like to have their interest and input to enable us to find better ways to make lectures, as mentioned by Dean Yoshino and Prof. Yamori.

Mr. Kazumasa Fukada: We are trying to boost interest among young people by qualifying the risks that potentially exist in their daily lives. For instance, we focus on risk management on common and avoidable liability matters such as bicycle accidents, recent social problems in Japan, and car traffic accidents that occur shortly after new drivers are awarded their driving license. That is very everyday life, they notice.

Ms. Anna Zelentsova: Thank you very much. My next question is to Mr. Hiroshi Ohata. You mentioned already that the elderly have specific issues, and I agree with Ms. Messy that there is one very important issue of fraud and also the issue of different types of manipulation of elderly people that some financial institutions or non-financial institutions use.

What do you think is the biggest risk for elderly people and how to address it, especially on this fraud issue, how to help them? Because in the Russian Federation, elderly people often have very high levels of trust in people and not enough knowledge. That is why sometimes mobile telephone and financial fraud is especially aimed at elderly people. How can you advise to deal with it?

Mr. Hiroshi Ohata: I would say one of the risks that those people face is that their decision-making ability would become impaired. So there is a possibility that they run down or lose their financial assets. For example, according to the Financial Literacy Map in Japan, elderly people should understand the adult guardian system. We have an adult guardian system in Japan, as have other countries. The adult guardian supports the elderly people's judgment to manage their financial assets. In addition, the FSA revised its supervisory guidelines in 2013 in order to protect them. For example, the FSA encourages financial institutions to amend their internal rules for soliciting elderly people and monitors their compliance. The FSA education staff and supervising staff share the information with a view to improving the FSA action.

Ms. Anna Zelentsova: Thank you very much and my last question is to Mr. Miles Larbey, about women, of course. As a woman thinking about retirement savings, my question is, who do you think are the best teachers for women? As you said, who would women listen to and how could they reach us to teach us about financial literacy?

Mr. Miles Larbey: Well, perhaps you should be answering your own question.

Ms. Anna Zelentsova: Exactly, next one.

Mr. Miles Larbey: You can tell me if I get it wrong. I mean I think that women and men like to listen to people in terms of experts, trusted figures. That could be media commentators, it could be financial experts and journalists and certainly we work with some of those in terms of some of our media campaigns and so on. With our new project we are building in partnership with the Office for Women, we hope to make use of the

Minister for Women in Australia. Now whether people listen to her, I do not know, but she certainly gets a lot of media attention.

But as I said, particularly the distribution of the resources we develop, we will be looking to work with as many community groups and NGOs as possible. So in Australia there is a network of what are called women's alliances all around the country which are essentially, as I say, largely NGOs, community groups, and local government organizations that come together and provide assistance and support, and information services, and so on. So we will be looking to work with those.

So I think in many respects it is the same for everyone—you want to listen to someone who you trust and who you feel has got some expertise that is worth listening to. I suppose, to add to that, as I said in my presentation, but this is not confined to women, we make as much use of real life case studies as possible and we have got a series of videos that are essentially women in different financial situations, one of whom is talking about retirement, just talking about their experience with their money issues, life events that they have experienced and how they dealt with them, and then what information and assistance they got.

Like I say, social media, we did not know this when we started, but our Facebook community is 75% women. Now I do not know actually if that is reflective of Facebook usage altogether or something specific about the topics that we are talking about through our social media channels, but it seems to be a really good way to reach that group.

Ms. Anna Zelentsova: Thank you very much, just one comment here. I think yes, but speaking about Facebook, as I am also a great fan of Facebook, I think that we women more easily say that we do not know something and discuss it. It is more difficult for men, probably, to recognize it and ask questions, especially in public. So maybe this is one of the reasons, but it is just my guess. Thank you very much again to everybody.

Ms. Flore-Anne Messy: Thank you very much, Mr. Larbey. I actually have a follow-up question, because when we worked on women within the INFE, one of the good practices that some of the countries identified is the importance of role models—not only women who had difficulties and managed to overcome them, but also women who are successful, speak about their success and how managing their financial life made them successful. So I was wondering whether you were also trying to play this card.

Mr. Miles Larbey: Yes, certainly. I mean I guess that part of the reason for the approach with the real life stories is that people have experienced that event, although not in every case. How did they succeed financially, how did they get to the point where they were in control financially? But, like I said, there are a lot of these people who appeal to both men and women. There are a number of leading female money journalists in Australia who have got quite a following both through traditional and social media, so we work with them, they are trusted figures and, I guess certainly as far as money is concerned, are role models. So I could not agree more, yes.

Ms. Flore-Anne Messy: Thank you. I know we have exceeded our allocated time, but we have been speaking a lot in the panel and you have been very patient and quiet in the audience. So yes, I see many raised hands. First the gentleman. Thank you.

Open Floor Discussion

Audience member: Good evening, I am from India. We work with mutual societies, basically focusing on women. India is a part of emerging markets and also part of BRICS—Brazil, Russian Federation, India, People's Republic of China, and South Africa. But the challenge is totally different given the social and cultural context. We are targeting women. So increasingly the challenge is that, as finances move toward digital, there is increasingly more digitizing. Two challenges—one is on the youth side and one concerns women who are working.

With respect to women, the challenge is to raise that level, not only the financial level but also the digital level, how we are going to do that? Because 95% of the population in India now has mobile phones, we are slowly enabling regulation, moving toward mobile-phone-based financial transactions. So the challenge is in the digital part. Financial education in isolation may not help and we need to think about digital literacy concomitantly. So that is the picture.

Ms. Flore-Anne Messy: So this is more of a comment. Is there a question here?

Audience member: Yes. There is also I think a re-strategizing of our approach, some kind of a suggestion. So the youth, particularly the online community, the Facebook community, display a lemming type of behavior, high-risk taking. So we need to have consumer protection from the perspective of sellers beware and buyers beware. So as a policy recommendation, how do we really work on the supply side where there is this weakness of the youth for taking high risks with high returns? This is where another dilemma is coming, where the youth are taking high risks, but then we need to also educate them about the kind of risks associated with that, and about online and also high risk products, derivatives, and so on. Without knowledge, some of them are trapped by the supply side. That is the issue I think that we need to address concomitantly. I think we need to work on that in particular, this is very important.

Ms. Flore-Anne Messy: Yes, thank you. I think these were two comments, but I think, indeed, digital literacy is important, especially in a country like India, or any other country where mobile banking or digital finance is being used to increase the level of financial inclusion. On your second comment, I believe you were saying that the level of information, especially on sophisticated investment products that are very risky, should be improved in many cases, so to make sure that the consumers get the information that not only the return is high, but the risks are very high as well. Is that your comment and is there any reaction in the panel about these two comments?

Ms. Anna Zelentsova: I can say a few words on the first comment about digital finance. In the G20 financial inclusion platform and global partnership for financial inclusion, we specially created a subgroup to focus more on markets and payments and digital finance last year. This issue of digital finance is one of the key priorities for the G20 financial inclusion platform for the next five years. We just developed a new financial inclusion action plan and especially focused, as you mentioned, on financial consumer protection and financial literacy, what kind of specific policies we have relating to digital finance. Some risks or some issues are the same, universal for other financial products, but some are specific for digital, so we will focus on policy responses in this area this year and next year. Hopefully that will provide some solutions.

Ms. Flore-Anne Messy: Yes, please.

Audience member: Thank you very much. I am from the Azerbaijan Micro-finance Association. First of all, I would like to thank all the panelists and my question will be for the FSA representative. I wonder if you also are considering providing education for financial institutions to promote responsible lending. And if yes, what are the materials and are they available for replication in other countries or not? Thank you very much.

Mr. Hiroshi Ohata: Excuse me, what do you mean by responsible lending?

Audience member: I mean do you provide financial education for the employees of financial institutions? So that when they provide financial services to low-income people, they can take into account the importance of financial education for their clients.

Mr. Hiroshi Ohata: The FSA provides financial education to the people in the regional area and in high schools or universities. So we do not dispatch our lecturers to the companies.

Mr. Miles Larbey: I can add to that. In Australia in 2011, a new statutory responsible lending regime was introduced which places obligations on providers of credit in terms of assessing the consumer's capacity to repay, whether the loan is likely to trigger financial hardship and so on. So we regulate those provisions of the law in the credit market. We do not provide education to the providers, but we do have a very substantial piece of guidance which is effectively a similar thing, to explain to providers of credit and credit services how we think they need to comply with the responsible lending laws, including a series of case studies and examples for different lending situations where this conduct might be deemed to be compliant with the law, but this conduct might be problematic. If you are interested in that, I can send that to you.

Dean Naoyuki Yoshino: I think I just want to add about a new Japanese law implemented a few years ago. One cannot borrow more money than one-third of one's annual income. We have a registration system so money lenders can find out how much money an individual is borrowing in total. Since then, default losses on loans from individuals have drastically diminished.

Ms. Flore-Anne Messy: Can I ask a follow-up question? I am interested in this responsible lending as well. Does it apply to all types of loans or only long-term ones, this one-third of income rule?

Dean Naoyuki Yoshino: I think it is all types of loans except for housing loans. Housing loans, that is different; this applies to consumer loans.

Ms. Flore-Anne Messy: One-third is already a lot for consumer loans.

Audience member: I may have a follow-up question to Dean Yoshino. Are there any sanctions if you are able to track which financial institution violated this? So can you see which institution did it and what are the sanctions if the financial institution failed in meeting this? Thank you.

Dean Naoyuki Yoshino: Yes. There are I think three levels of monitoring. One is the money lenders association themselves; they are watching whether some institution has violated the rules, and, if so, they monitor that institution. The second level is local government under the FSA and the Ministry of Finance. Then lastly, the FSA will check, so there are three levels of monitoring. If an institution is in serious violation, their business will be stopped, which is the toughest sanction.

Audience member: Do you have some control of that, because it could be possible that people wanted to borrow and could not because of the ceiling, so they just went to the informal market.

Dean Naoyuki Yoshino: We used to have a very big informal market. Then we tried to move everything into the formal system as much as we could, to get it into the regulatory framework. According to our surveys, that informal market has drastically diminished after we implemented the law stipulating that one cannot borrow more than one-third of one's annual income. The black market is very difficult to monitor, but according to our survey, it is now much, much smaller.

Ms. Flore-Anne Messy: Thank you. Yes, please, you have been very patient.

Audience member: Two short questions. One is for Prof. Yamori. If a plan is started for teachers in Japan so they study experiences of asset allocation and investment, then they might become more interested in finance. What do you think about this idea? Second, for Mr. Ohata, for elderly people, face-to-face neutral financial consulting is important along with financial education. What do you think about this point?

Prof. Nobuyoshi Yamori: Yes, first of all, according to the survey, many teachers believe that recently finance has become a very important subject in schools. But it should be noted that we send our questionnaire to the teachers who are actually in charge of teaching finance and there are a lot of teachers teaching other subjects. So realistically speaking, it is not the majority of all teachers who say that finance is important. We only know that the teachers in charge of the civics or home economics classes say that finance is important.

Mr. Hiroshi Ohata: As I mentioned, we advise people, including elderly people, through our helpline and this is my opinion: face-to-face consultation is useful, but we cannot cover all people in Japan. I think there are many problems that should be solved.

Ms. Flore-Anne Messy: Yes, thank you. Yes, indeed, face-to-face is one of the most expensive ways to provide financial education. Having said that, if you target people in great difficulties, it is probably one of the best ways to help them. I know there have been a number of surveys, maybe including in Australia, where you try to assess the trade-off between the different types of intervention depending on the cost and the value-added. Would you like to say something about this, Mr. Larbey?

Mr. Miles Larbey: That is right, I mean certainly there are a number of programs operating in Australia which involve a face-to-face component and they tend to be focused very much on financially vulnerable disadvantaged consumers, which may include some elderly consumers, but they are not specific for the elderly. They are often linked to match savings programs and certainly the results of those programs are very encouraging for the participants in terms of encouraging savings behavior and perhaps reaching savings goals that the participants may have never achieved before in their lives. But they are usually small-scale because they are resource-intensive, they require trainers or facilitators who know what they are doing and so there certainly is a trade-off.

Ms. Flore-Anne Messy: Thank you very much, Mr. Larbey. Any other questions from the audience? Yes, please. Again, short questions because now we are really running out of time.

Audience member: I have just two small things to say. One, as Prof. Yoshino said and in our country experience also, when banks were asked to spend money on financial education, in their books all the advertisement expenses were shown as financial education expenses. So is there an ethical conflict in such a case? That is number one.

Number two, when we are defining target audiences of financial education, what about the 2 billion people who do not have formal financial access at all? Do they not need a very well-tailored financial education? When we talk about them, we only are talking about micro-finance instruments to reach them, but as we saw in the last presentation, the cost of funds going to them is something like 20%–30%. That means the rate of return for the survival of SMEs should be like 100% in each year if that is also their bread-earning enterprise.

If we are saying media is one of the very effective vehicles for financial education, I think we should include the mainstream media board in the financial education package. Three different issues I have raised. Thank you.

Ms. Flore-Anne Messy: Thank you, I see three, and I would not say they are small questions. I think we can spend dinner over this, but if there is some quick reaction on the first question? Yes, please.

Dean Naoyuki Yoshino: I think you are talking about conflicts of interest, but many associations including life insurance and the non-life insurance and banking industries have their own education systems. Most of the time they are very neutral and they have some strong connections with universities and schools. So I think there are two levels of education—one is purely neutral, that by the central bank and the FSA. Second, the financial industry knows their own products much better, so education should be provided by them as well. If they start to talk about their own products, probably it is better to say this is my own opinion, but I would like to explain some of the products. So I think the level of their education should be up to some point neutral, then if they go into specific products, they should honestly say this is just our promotion and so on. This would be a very good way to avoid conflicts of interest.

Ms. Flore-Anne Messy: Thank you, Dean Yoshino. I think Mr. Larbey, you wanted to add something?

Mr. Miles Larbey: I was just going to refer to the OECD guidelines, but certainly in Australia we have promoted those for private sector organizations that want to get involved in financial education.

Ms. Flore-Anne Messy: Yes, the guidelines are specifically dealing with this conflict of interest and providing a list of criteria that private institutions should apply if they want to say they deliver financial education and not pure marketing. Last question and then the rest will be for dinner.

Audience member: I just have a small question. I am from Bank Indonesia. I have a question for the presenter from BoJ and FSA. Could you please explain a little bit more the difference between the role of BoJ and FSA in terms of education programs?

Ms. Ryoko Okazaki: BoJ is mainly supporting the independent organization, which I can explain as the Central Council for Financial Services Information, which is an organization consisting of the representatives of almost all the national associations of financial institutions and economic organizations and women's organizations and experts from academic society. The Deputy Governor of Bank of Japan is also a member of the Central Council. The secretary has a new plan every fiscal year, which includes various forms of promoting financial education.

We also ran the Committee for Promotion of Financial Education with the FSA. The FSA also provides information on its website, and the CCFSI also has rich contents on its website. The FSA developed educational materials several years ago and we are also providing educational materials. We are all the time cooperating with each other, with all the national associations of financial institutions and the experts from educational society and academics.

Ms. Flore-Anne Messy: Thank you very much. Again, I think it is also a good subject for dinner because there are indeed many activities by these different institutions. But what is important is that you are cooperating and coordinating at the national level.

Financial Education in Japan: Challenges Presented by the Aging Population and Declining Birthrate

Kikuo Iwata, Deputy Governor of the Bank of Japan: Good morning, ladies and gentlemen. I am Kikuo Iwata from the Bank of Japan. I am most pleased to have all of you here in Tokyo, to discuss financial education. I believe that sharing the insight and knowledge gained by some countries will benefit participants from other ones. I would like to thank the organizers and all involved.

The Bank of Japan serves as the secretariat of the Central Council for Financial Services Information, which promotes financial education in Japan. As a member of the council, I feel that financial education has become increasingly important worldwide, particularly after the recent global financial crisis. I also think that country-specific factors and historical background have had considerable influence.

Today, I would like to talk about financial literacy in Japan, including the current situation, challenges, and issues in promoting financial education. The country has been undergoing demographic changes, particularly of the aging population and declining birthrate. Indeed, it is aging more rapidly than most countries. I hope that our experience with addressing these financial literacy matters will offer you some insight.

1. Need for Financial Literacy Arising from Demographic Changes

An aging population and declining birthrate represent the greatest social and economic issues in Japan. The average life expectancy is 80 years for men and 86 years for women, and the population's longevity is one of the highest in the world. Over the past six decades, life expectancy has increased by more than 20 years for both men and women. While we should welcome the increase, maintaining one's living standard over a longer retirement period has become a crucial issue. In addition, with the declining birthrate, the proportion of people aged 65 years and older is expected to rise to nearly 30% by 2020. Considering the large burden borne by the working-age generations, the role of public pensions will become smaller.

In other words, each individual's efforts to achieve financial independence in their retirement period have become more important. Encouraging elderly people to work longer is one important factor, but so is improving financial literacy. Starting lifetime planning while still young and reserving assets for retirement will help.

2. Changes in Financial Behavior and Challenges Presented by the Aging Population and Declining Birthrate

The need for improved financial literacy is gradually taking hold in Japan. In the council's survey, we ask about the "purpose of holding financial assets." The reply chosen most often had long been "preparation for illness and unexpected emergency." But in 2013, this changed for the first time in its 60-year history to "funds for life during my retirement period." This is symbolic for Japan, which has a well-developed public pension system.

The financial behavior of Japanese people has changed accordingly. Households' financial assets[a] have increased by around 20% over the last decade; that is, the period before and after the global financial crisis. Notably, the amount held by people aged 60 years and older has reached 25 million yen per household. This is almost the same level as the "target amount of funds you regard as necessary" in the survey. Financial assets are being accumulated to ensure a stable living standard over an individual's retirement period.

---

[a] The financial assets here are financial instruments, including bank deposits and postal savings, that are held for investment or reserved for future use. Funds held for business purposes and daily use are excluded.

However, there are worrisome signs that financial literacy associated with lifetime planning has been undermined.

As I mentioned earlier, households' financial assets have been growing. However, at the same time, the number of households that do not have such assets has been increasing recently. This trend has been observed in a wide range of income groups, including the high-income group. The backgrounds to this are varied, and problems related to financial literacy represent one of the factors. One example is a weaker awareness of the importance of lifetime planning.

There are various concerns regarding children as well. In this affluent society that is undergoing demographic changes and rapid progress in technology, children could lose their sense of the value of money. For example, we have the so-called "six pocket problem." This refers to a phenomenon in which a child is indulged with money given by the parents and grandparents of both the father and mother. Another is the "invisible money problem"; that is, a situation in which a child does not feel that they actually paid a price for something, given the increasing use of electronic money. In both cases, children have fewer opportunities to realize, through the firsthand experience of using physical money, that there are limits to the money we can spend.

We must keep up with these developments, as lifestyles and values have become diverse and everyday life is more dependent on and convenient with technology. However, we still need to understand that there are limits to the goods we can own and the money we can spend, so as to make sure that we make appropriate choices on daily consumption, financial transactions, and lifetime planning. We need to be aware of significant financial literacy factors—namely, the scarcity of money and resources as well as lifetime planning. Creating such awareness through financial education is challenging, but we cannot avoid this task.

Another issue that warrants attention is the rapid increase in financial fraud targeted at elderly people. I feel very sorry for the victims of such crimes. At the same time, the increase in financial fraud suggests that we need to strengthen the financial literacy of elderly people. The victims of financial fraud might have been caught off-guard. If they had had a little more financial literacy, they might not have been deceived. On the basis of our survey, we deem that elderly people generally have more confidence in their own financial literacy compared to other age groups. But in fact, they tend to have insufficient literacy. We should close the gap between high confidence and low literacy.

We need to check and control daily payments, manage portfolios in line with lifetime plans, and always confirm the points to check when concluding a contract. Enhancing financial literacy in this way will be effective in guarding against financial fraud and, at the same time, developing efficient asset formation.

3.   Initiatives Taken in Japan

In 2013, Japan's Financial Services Agency compiled a report that showed the future direction of financial education, drawing on the experience of the global financial crisis. It proposed to emphasize literacy for financial behavior and focus on the basics of financial literacy to make it easier to learn. Based on this report, our council has been working to set standards and specify the contents of financial education by age group, and has formulated the Financial Literacy Map.

The council also provides easy-to-understand teaching materials, pamphlets, and DVDs in cooperation with financial industry groups and other relevant organizations. In particular, we have pamphlets for middle-aged and elderly people, who must consider how to maintain their living standard over their retirement period as an immediate, practical issue. In cooperation with relevant organizations, the council also gives lectures to university students that place emphasis on fostering decision-making ability. Through these activities, it has been promoting more effective financial education for working-age generations to prepare them for later years.

In fiscal 2005, our council launched a campaign that aims to improve financial education at schools. It has developed the contents of such financial education by age group. The council also provides various teaching materials, including practical teaching cases for school children.

Indeed, to promote financial education activities more effectively, it is important to provide necessary information to people who are not interested in lifetime planning. It is also necessary to devise ways of encouraging them to take appropriate actions so as to maintain lifetime financial independence. These are difficult tasks, but it is vital to make people understand, through easy-to-understand and accessible means, that financial literacy reduces risks in their future lives. It is also essential to communicate to the public in a more effective manner by using behavioral economics insights.

4. Conclusion

The Bank of Japan will continue to promote financial education through the activities of the council. We will maintain close cooperation with the Financial Services Agency and relevant organizations. Through our efforts, we hope that Japanese people can continue to live stable, affluent lives despite the aging population and declining birthrate.

I would like to conclude my speech by expressing our commitment to stronger cooperation with those of you who have gathered here today from the OECD and various countries around the world.

Thank you for your kind attention.

Financial Inclusion, Financial Regulation, and Financial Education in Asia

Ganeshan Wignaraja, Director of Research, ADBI: Welcome to this session on financial inclusion, financial regulation, and financial education in Asia. In the previous sessions, we looked quite a bit at the experience of financial education in developed countries. In this session, we are going to shift more to developing economies in Asia, because the issues may be somewhat different. Asia is growing at 6% per year, but poverty and inequality remain pressing challenges. Financial education thus becomes an important way to facilitate inclusive growth.

This session considers four interesting cases from Southeast Asia—Indonesia, the Philippines, Thailand, and Viet Nam, as well as Pakistan from South Asia. The real question for this session is what are the applicable lessons from experiences in Asia for developing approaches to financial education. Answering this question means focusing on issues such as diagnostics, coverage of target groups, national strategies, and implementation issues. So we want this session to distill the real lessons on the ground from an interesting set of countries.

To address these issues, we have an excellent panel of Asian experts here. These include: Dr. Muliaman Hadad, who is Chairman of the Financial Services Authority of Indonesia; Dr. Saeed Ahmed, who is Director of Agriculture, Credit and Microfinance Department of the State Bank of Pakistan; Attorney Prudence Kasala, who is Head of Consumer Protection Department, Central Bank of the Philippines; Mr. Nguyen Vinh Hung, who is Deputy Director General, International Department of the State Bank of Vietnam; and Ms. Nichaya Kosolwongse, who is Visiting Fellow, Asian Financial Partnership Center of the Financial Services

Agency (FSA) of Japan and who is also from the Securities and Exchange Commission (SEC) of Thailand.

I am going to kindly request each of the panelists to speak for 10–12 minutes. After the presentations, I will pose a question to each of them and then we will open the discussion to the floor so we can have a very interactive session. Dr. Hadad, please, you have the floor for 10–12 minutes.

Financial Inclusion, Financial Regulation, and Financial Education in Asia: Case of Indonesia

Muliaman D. Hadad, Chairman Financial Services Authority Indonesia: Thank you, Chairman. Good morning, everyone. Allow me to take this opportunity to thank ADBI for this very important occasion. I would like to take this opportunity to share our real views as a financial services regulator and supervisor in Indonesia. From this point of view, it is very clear that what I would like to say is very much related to the view of the regulators and supervisors and to how we are able to support the government as a whole and other stakeholders to improve not only education but also access to finance.

Because for most developing markets, I think there are two important areas to take into consideration. The first one is about education, financial literacy, and related areas—there are a lot of initiatives coming in these areas. The second issue is very much about financial capability—access to finance and financial inclusion. I mean there are two—I try to divide it into two different areas—that seem to me are very important.

Let me just provide you with some indicators. Financial literacy in Indonesia is still considerably low compared with perhaps our neighbors in Asia. The World Bank conducted surveys in Indonesia in 2010. It is really very clear that the literacy level still needs to be improved further, because if I may say, around 22% of adults in Indonesia have a formal linkage to formal financial institutions, but the rest is still very informal. That is why financial literacy is really an issue in Indonesia.

On the other hand, as I mentioned earlier, financial access or access to finance is really quite an issue as well. In particular, all of us in Indonesia, including the government, would like to see that access improve. Improving access to finance is really one of the major initiatives to improve people's welfare, as is the poverty alleviation program. That is why these two areas are the top priority in Indonesia.

Being a unified regulator or supervisor, because you may already be aware that the Indonesian FSA is basically supervising all financial sectors in Indonesia—banking, capital markets, and non-bank financial institutions—we have a cross-industry view, which gives us a considerable advantage to stimulate the financial inclusion program. Firstly, the financial inclusion program and performance monitoring can be conducted more comprehensively and integrally in the matters of supply and demand and infrastructure. So we can view them from the supply side, the demand side, and the infrastructure side to support all these things. Secondly, in line with our role in education and protection over financial consumer and society, the Indonesian FSA has to prepare policy options to improve overall financial inclusion, especially in stimulating the demand side of the market.

Let me brief you a little bit on the inclusion of the rural regions. As you may be aware, or we are all aware here, financial inclusion is now a global agenda. Our country has adopted financial inclusion as an essential pillar of the national strategy for reducing the rising income disparity between rural and urban areas. This commitment was followed by the declaration of national strategy for financial inclusion at the Association of Southeast Asian Nations (ASEAN) Summit in 2010. Indonesia's economic growth is expected to increase to 8% in 2018. Currently, we have more than 250 million people, and around 60 million microenterprise businesses in Indonesia.

Of course, judging from the overall potential for growth in Indonesia, Indonesia has a lot of potential to stimulate demand for financial products and services. As I mentioned earlier, the World Bank survey found that a still considerably big chunk of the Indonesian people has low financial literacy. Such a low level of financial inclusion in Indonesia of course offers an opportunity to create a more inclusive financial system which promotes the greater participation of the community in the financial services industry in line with the objective of economic growth and poverty alleviation.

In response to this, the Indonesian FSA has initiated several programs to improve the level of financial inclusion and to increase the access to finance for Indonesian people, such as comprehensive nationwide financial education activities and the introduction of branchless banking. We just launched our branchless banking this year. We hired more than 30,000 new agents to support branchless banking, as well as harnessing the society in general by organizing a financial inclusion competition and other activities.

According to research that we believe is very important, for inclusion to be successful, more effort is needed to address the gaps in understanding financial inclusion, particularly its results. We see that there are at least three aspects that occupy our attention. First is the quality of regulatory policies. Evidence is limited on which policies work best in each country. These need to be verified to ensure that policies are indeed addressing the right problems of financial access in the country. Second, it is also important to have a positive enabling environment for promoting financial inclusion. Policies that support financial inclusion have to be closely connected with the pursuit of macroeconomic stability. Third, greater financial inclusion is only possible if undertaken responsibly. Inasmuch as inclusion is about increasing the capability to use financial services, it is crucial that those who are directly affected are financially literate and capable.

Regarding promoting better lifetime planning through financial education, I would like to briefly touch on this issue. The low level of financial literacy among children and adolescents limit their ability to make good financial decisions. It is a very important topic as well. This is where the role of government is crucial. Authorities and agencies need to work together to improve the overall financial literacy of society, which should begin at the early age in order to provide them with the necessary dividend. That is why this is also one of our top priority areas—attracting individuals and households engaged in the informal sector to the formal financial sector.

On the topic related to dealing with the informal lenders, I would like to say something on this. Limited access to the banking sector can become an entry point for informal creditors who impose very high interest rates. Considering these are very important issues, the Indonesian government in

2013 enacted a new law on microfinance institutions. Now the Indonesian FSA is also responsible for supervising microfinance in Indonesia. This regulation issued by the Indonesian FSA is formulated to provide stronger regulatory standards, governance, and consumer protection to ensure that microfinance can contribute to the empowerment of those with low incomes.

Again it is very important for us at least to recognize the importance of very important factors. In particular, if we would like to include small and medium-sized enterprises (SMEs) in our financial inclusion, we would like to see that SMEs have adequate levels of personal entrepreneurial competencies, SMEs have an appropriate level of understanding on the life cycle of funding, SMEs understand and can manage financial risk, SMEs also understand legal issues, and SMEs understand the range of legal recourse it can resort to when necessary. This is a very important topic that should be taken into consideration by all stakeholders who are really concerned about inclusion as far as the SMEs are concerned.

Lastly, we are seeing a greater awareness of the importance of financial inclusion and then I do believe that a regulator cannot be left alone in dealing with this. Achieving financial inclusion and a financially literate society requires long-term changes and a committed engagement of diverse stakeholders. In closing, allow me to convey my sincere gratitude to all of you for being able to attend this very important occasion. Thank you very much.

Dr. Ganeshan Wignaraja: Dr. Hadad, thank you for a comprehensive presentation. Dr. Ahmed, please.

Advancing Financial Inclusion through Financial Education in Pakistan

Saeed Ahmed, Director, Agricultural Credit & Microfinance Department, State Bank of Pakistan: Thank you, Dr. Wignaraja. Good morning, ladies and gentlemen. It is a pleasure to be here in Tokyo to present Pakistan's experience with financial inclusion, financial regulation, and financial literacy. In the interest of time, I will skip the initial slides that focus mainly on the importance of financial literacy and how it is related to financial inclusion. We have already heard presentations from eminent speakers highlighting the importance of financial literacy and its different dimensions. This morning also, we heard from the Deputy Governor of the Bank of Japan on the importance of the topic.

In order to keep within the time allotted, I will focus on Pakistan's experience. But having said that, let me make a few initial statements. There is a global recognition that financial inclusion is an important ingredient of economic and social progress, because access to appropriate financial services helps micro and small businesses better manage their affairs, it spurs local economic activity, and at the macro level, the depth of financial intermediation is associated with faster economic growth and less income inequality. Therefore, in the context of developing countries, the low levels of financial literacy and financial capability form the biggest barrier to financial inclusion.

The case of Pakistan is the same as that of Indonesia, as we just heard from the presentation from Indonesia—Pakistan's level of financial exclusion is very high. So financial inclusion remains a top priority on the government's agenda as well as that of the central bank of Pakistan.

Let me give you a bit of country context. Pakistan is a medium-sized, lower-middle-income country with a population of about 188 million. Over 100 million of the population is below the age of 25 years, so we have a large population which is young. Therefore, we have to focus on developing financial capability to create financially responsible citizens in the future. Basic literacy is also a major problem in Pakistan, with a 61% literacy rate, and in terms of gross domestic product (GDP) Pakistan ranks 44th in the world and annual GDP growth is between 4% and 5%.

Pakistan's financial sector, and particularly the banking sector which comprises over 80% of the assets of the financial sector, has shown resilience, profitability, and dynamism, even in the aftermath of the financial crisis of 2008. The biggest issue in the financial sector in Pakistan is that it remains restricted in its outreach—56% of the adult population in Pakistan does not have access to financial services.

To start with, we did a survey in collaboration with the World Bank, the Skill Development Council, Asian Development Bank, and other stakeholders. The survey was completed in 2007 and 2008. It showed

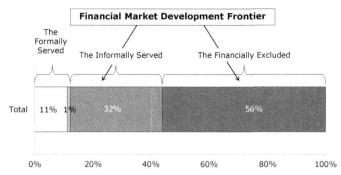

56% of the adult population doesn't have access to financial services

- Currently the repeat A2F survey is underway and the estimates of formally served are expected to be above 20%
- Lack of financial capability is one of the leading causes of financial exclusion

Figure 4.1   Financial inclusion landscape of Pakistan
Source: State Bank of Pakistan. Access to Finance Survey (2008).

that 56% of the population is totally financially excluded (Figure 4.1). Another 32% of the population is informally served. So only 12% of the population was being served by formal financial providers. That is the formal financial market and you need to bring that 32% of the population into the formal financial system.

The important point is that the lack of financial literacy and capability is one of the leading causes of financial exclusion. This emerged from the findings of the Access to Finance Survey in 2008. This is the reason financial inclusion has assumed a very high priority on the agenda of the central bank. The State Bank of Pakistan is an active player within the international community. We are a founding member of the Alliance for Financial Inclusion. We work very closely with international development agencies, the OECD, and the G20. We contributed to the development of the G20's principle of innovative financial inclusion through the forum of Alliance for Financial Inclusion (AFI). The State Bank is represented on the working groups of Alliance for Financial Inclusion and I happen to be the co-chair of AFI's working group on consumer empowerment and market conduct.

Regarding financial literacy, let me share with you the financial literacy gaps. About 40% of the financially excluded population reported a lack of understanding of financial products as the main reason for financial exclusion. This emerged from the Access to Finance Survey of 2008. More than half of the adult population, 56%, is saving, with the majority using informal means. Females seem to be saving less than males—53% versus 60%.

We are repeating the Access to Finance Survey in 2015, which is showing marked improvement over 2008 results. Interestingly, during the initial pilot stage, it was found that not having enough information about bank accounts is the biggest hurdle in getting a bank account. This is followed by the lack of technical ability and understanding of how to use a bank account. So lack of financial literacy is a major barrier toward advancing financing inclusion.

So this is our financial inclusion strategy (Figure 4.2). The State Bank of Pakistan, in collaboration with the World Bank, has just completed the first national financial inclusion strategy. We did have an implicit financial inclusion strategy for the last seven years. The State Bank had been implementing various supply-side initiatives to advance financial

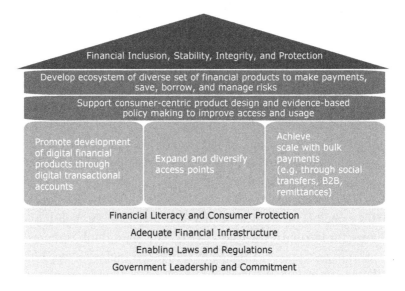

Figure 4.2   Financial inclusion objectives and vision
Source: State Bank of Pakistan.

inclusion in Pakistan, but we did not have an explicit national financial inclusion strategy. So the strategy has just been finalized and as you can see in Figure 4.2, financial literacy and consumer protection are an important pillar of our national financial inclusion strategy, in addition to the government commitment, laws and regulations, and financial infrastructure.

The key enablers include digital financial products through regional transaction accounts. Pakistan is promoting branchless banking in a big way. Pakistan is one of the fastest growing markets for branchless banking. Let me share with you some statistics. Over 22 million transactions are taking place every month through branchless banking providers and the average size of branchless banking is just $50. So that shows that through mobile phone banking, we are reaching out to the millions of underserved people. Branchless banking is our delivery strategy because by using brick-and-mortar approaches we would not have been able to reach out to the millions of underserved people. So we are using alternative delivery channels.

In addition to the 12,500 bank branches all over the country, over 186,000 access points have emerged over the last couple of years. These are the branchless banking agents. So we are providing agent-based banking. These are our key enablers and, of course, the overarching aim is to ensure financial inclusion, stability, integrity, and consumer protection. These are the four policy objectives that the central bank is pursuing.

So what is our approach to financial literacy? I think this is now the hot topic. We have a three-pronged approach to improving financial literacy in Pakistan as a complement to financial inclusion and consumer protection. First, we have created second-tier microfinance banks within the regulated sector to serve the lower-income population. These second-tier microfinance banks are an alternative to conventional banking, to serve the low-income and the marginalized segments of our society. So we are giving these regulated microfinance providers specific directions to advance financial literacy.

Second, supply-side initiatives have been undertaken to fill gaps, which can marginalize financially illiterate customers. Third, demand side. We are addressing demand-side issues. We have taken capacity building initiatives to promote financial literacy to improve demand-side variables, because without financial literacy and capability, consumer protection regulations cannot adequately protect the consumers. So to address financial literacy issues, the demand side has to come hand in hand with the regulations. That is the critical message.

Since the customers of microfinance banks often lack awareness about their rights and obligations, we have given instructions to microfinance banks to develop a mandatory financial literacy program for their customers. So that has been made mandatory because we believe that in the initial phase of microfinance sector development, we did not have very stringent consumer protection regulations, but now that the microfinance sector has achieved maturity, we have revised microfinance banking and consumer protection regulations in 2014, specifically focusing on financial literacy, transparency, and disclosure. Microfinance banks have been advised to set up a complaint register mechanism and they also have to develop a code for debt collection practices, which has to be approved by their board of directors.

The financial literacy program that each microfinance bank has to develop at minimum should cover charges, fees, interest rate calculations, repayment schedules, customers' obligations, and other terms and conditions of all financial services. So the program, the financial literacy program, should educate customers about lodging complaints and track the resolution of complaints. Because it is equally important that the financially illiterate clients of microfinance banks know where to lodge a complaint and how to track its progress.

In addition to this, since Pakistan suffers from low levels of financial literacy, it is critical for microfinance providers to be transparent in their pricing as well as uphold the rights of consumers. In this context, client protection initiatives have recently been undertaken to not only mandate all the microfinance banks to transparently disclose their pricing, but also to ensure convergence of industry client protection practices as per SMART guidelines. So the State Bank of Pakistan has supported the Pakistan Microfinance Network in partnership with Microfinance Transparency and Smart Campaign to launch these supply-side initiatives.

Now this is important. As I said, the State Bank has made a number of supply-side interventions, initiatives, to advance financial inclusion in the country, but what was missing was a demand-side solution to advance financial inclusion, one that tends to impart financial education and awareness to the customers.

So the State Bank of Pakistan designed a financial literacy program (Figure 4.3). This was the first ever national financial literacy program that was developed by a state bank and the objective was to impart knowledge and understanding of financial concepts, products, and services and also to bring about behavioral change among the masses toward money management practices. The financial literacy program was developed under Asian Development Bank funding of improved access to financial services. The State Bank of Pakistan created a platform to coordinate, design, and implement this program.

The steering committee that was formed to design and develop this program had representation from the Pakistan Banks' Association, the Microfinance Network, the education sector, and the Asian Development Bank. So it was important that all the key stakeholders were involved from the beginning. The curriculum and the content that was developed was disseminated through focused classroom training sessions. We conducted activity-based workshops all over the country and as street theaters and puppet shows are still very popular in Pakistan, the curriculum was

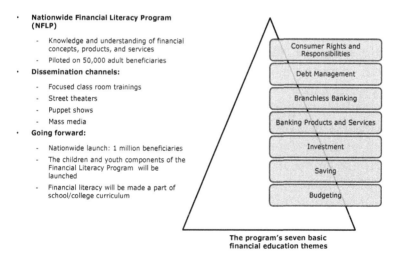

Figure 4.3   SBP demand-side initiative: National Financial Literacy Program
Source: State Bank of Pakistan.

disseminated through street theaters. They proved to be very interesting, so they conveyed the main messages on financial concepts and on different types of media and we also used mass media channels (TV and radio) to carry the headline messages.

The important thing was that initially we launched that program on a pilot basis. Through this pilot, we reached out to nearly 50,000 adult beneficiaries. They were all part of the low-income, unbanked population. We have just completed the independent assessment of the pilot program and we are now about to launch the national financial literacy program, aiming to reach out to 1 million direct beneficiaries through workshops. The children and youth component of the financial literacy program was not part of the pilot, but we intend to make it a part of the national rollout program.

The program content was developed around several basic themes: budgeting, savings, investments, banking products, and services. It was very important to give basic education, basic knowledge about branchless banking to the unbanked population, and then about debt management and consumer rights and responsibilities. So financial education needs to be tailored to the client's specific context. I am sharing a few slides, snapshots of the curriculum we designed for the national financial literacy program (Figure 4.4). This was specifically tailored for the target marketing. For example, why to save.

The curriculum was translated into regional languages—Urdu, Sindhi, Pashtun, and others. We use the pictorial handbooks to develop training material. Regarding mobile banking—again, it was important to talk to these people on their level about branchless banking.

So let me now just conclude my presentation with the lessons that we learned in developing and implementing the first national financial literacy program. Coordination is very important. I think it is very important to involve all the key players from the beginning. As I said, we involved all the key stakeholders from the banks' representatives, from the microfinance sector, and also from the education sector, to develop that program and monitor its progress over time. So that is how we created ownership for the success of the program.

Because financial education and financial literacy are all about customers, they have to be at the center stage. So the curriculum must be

Figure 4.4   Why save?
Source: State Bank of Pakistan (www.financialeducation.pk).

developed and adapted to their circumstances. We learned from the best financial education programs all over the world and we adapted them to suit our local context. Prior to that, we conducted a financial literacy gap survey to get feedback from financial consumers.

Also, any nationwide financial literacy program should follow an open structure, so there is room for the other stakeholders to join in. To give credibility to any national financial literacy program, it is important that the branding of the program should be neutral. The products and the institution should not have any marketing role in the financial literacy program. So the financial institutions can join in, but the branding should be kept neutral.

It is very important to monitor the results, and this came out in the discussions yesterday, that what cannot be measured cannot be improved.

So monitoring and evaluation is very important and, finally, leadership is very important. I think you have to involve all the stakeholders in the financial literacy program. Thank you.

Dr. Ganeshan Wignaraja: Thank you. Ms. Angelita Kasala, please.

Save Now or Pay Later: A Philippine Perspective on Financial Inclusion and Education

Prudence Angelita A. Kasala, Head of the Financial Consumer Protection Department, Bangko Sentral ng Pilipinas: Good morning, everyone. Given the time constraints, I will jump straight into my presentation. As a central banker, I believe that the Philippines is standing at a very important threshold, an inflection point where our sound economic fundamentals and consistent strong performance for the last five years can serve as a springboard that would finally catapult us to real and lasting progress.

For economic development to be truly meaningful, such development must translate to financial wellbeing of the individual Filipino, and to achieve that, the Bangko Sentral ng Pilipinas (BSP) undertook financial inclusion initiatives. The BSP crafted policies that are necessary for the regulatory environment to be conducive to offering financial products and services to the unbanked and the underserved. The BSP's work in this area has been consistently cited internationally. Our gains in financial inclusion are shown in Table 4.1.

While microfinance and other bank products have become easily accessible to Filipinos, data show, however, that overall usage of bank products, which include savings accounts, continues to remain low. For example, findings in the 2009 consumer finance survey showed that eight out of ten Filipinos actually do not have any bank accounts. Of those unbanked, 92.8% did not have enough money for bank deposits. Another interesting result of the survey is that one-fifth of Filipino households depend solely or partly on remittances to support their expenditure requirements. This just shows the importance of overseas Filipino workers in financially supported households in the Philippines, and as you know, you can find Filipinos almost anywhere.

The number of households with savings, however, has been increasing from 2009 to 2014, from 20% to 30%. However, for the third and fourth quarter of 2014, a survey on consumer savings showed that roughly only 25% of households have savings. Of that 25%, a significant 30% still keep their extra money in cooperatives and other credit associations, which are not regulated. Thus, it appears that, notwithstanding the wider availability of financial products, consumers have not availed themselves of such products and services.

What does that say? There seems to be an underlying issue of trust in the slow uptake of financial products. In one study, researchers reported a strong preference for cash, which could be attributed both to savings on taxes and a lack of awareness of and trust in financial products. For instance, news regarding people being scammed and defrauded clearly dampened the trust in available financial products and even the financial system. Clearly, the BSP should focus not only on the supply of financial products and services, but on the demand as well. The demand for financial products and services could be enhanced through financial education and consumer protection.

Table 4.1   Financial inclusion key data (2013–Q2 2014)

	2013	Q2 2014
Banking offices	9,884	10,073
ATMs	14,528	14,841
Deposit accounts	45.4 million	46.9 million
Total deposits	P7.6 trillion	P7.8 trillion
Micro-banking offices (MBOs)	465	501
Local government units (LGUs) without regular banking offices and served by MBOs	56	65
Micro-enterprise loan	P6 billion in 170 banks	P7.8 billion in 167 banks
Micro-deposits	P2.6 billion in 67 banks	P3.3 billion in 69 banks
Registered e-money accounts	26.7 million*	–

* In 2010, there were only 7.9 million e-money accounts.
Note: No. of LGUs is 1,634.
Source: Bangko Sentral ng Pilipinas

Consumer empowerment through financial education would provide the public with an understanding of the benefits of the available financial products and services, and rather than just being aware of the products' existence, the knowledge of what the products can do for them or how they can serve them will make consumers want to use them.

On the other hand, consumer protection would address concerns on potential frauds and scams, which usually permanently put people off from using financial products. Consumers need to feel safe and secure when they use a product. Consumers will only fully trust a product if they know that they are protected if anything beyond their control happens. They need to know that financial institutions are being monitored and regulated and that someone is looking out for their rights.

We firmly believe that financial inclusion, financial education, and consumer protection are three legs of a stool that could not stand if any of its legs were missing. As complementary initiatives to financial inclusion, the BSP saw the need to dedicate more supervisory resources to financial education and financial consumer protection. As I mentioned earlier, this is mainly due to the fact that financial inclusion targets the supply side, while financial education and consumer protection target the demand side.

We have personally experienced the challenges in financial education, as pointed out by our various panelists in this forum. How can it be easy to teach someone who believes that he is financially literate, but actually is not? Just to give you an idea on the disparity between self-perception of financial literacy and actual financial knowledge—a study of Filipinos in 2013 showed that while 20% believe that they are experts, when they took the test, no one scored above 90 and only 8% scored above 80 and 79% got below 70 or failed.

While we have worked on developing an instructor's guide for teaching financial education to elementary students, our public school teachers are grappling with their own issues of being burdened by personal or salary loans. So unlike in Japan where the problem is whether the teachers are academically competent, the teachers in the Philippines actually have their own financial woes to worry about.

We also recognize that a different audience requires a different approach, focus, and delivery mechanism based on the needs, interests, and preferences. This further complicates the process of developing and delivering materials and learning modules. Monitoring and impact evaluation remain a challenge as impact is best seen in the change in behavior, which is not only difficult to effect, but also difficult to measure. As we know, change in behavior is always difficult to measure and financial education can always be likened to physical exercise. We know that it is good for us, but it really takes discipline for us to engage in it.

Likewise, I think everyone is aware that financial education is a lifelong process and that for it to be meaningful, it has to be consistently or regularly administered. Take for example smoking or eating sweets. We know from a very young age that this is bad for health, and yet, maybe some of us are still smoking or still indulging in sweets. So change in behavior is very critical. In the same vein, we know that while it is good to save, when faced with the magical four-letter word—and we know what that magical four-letter word is, sale—our will collapses and we just spend unnecessarily.

Let us further complicate the challenges of financial education with the realities of retirement. One of the key messages in our educational modules is savings for retirement and again we share the same experience in other jurisdictions. We see the insufficiency of retirement pensions to meet daily basic needs. The highest pension for a private sector employee is 16,000 pesos or roughly $365, but the average monthly pension for a private sector employee is just 3,000 pesos or $67. The pension for government employees is roughly 10,000 pesos or approximately $220. These figures barely reach the monthly minimum wage.

We also see an increase in life expectancy—73 years for females and 67 for males. It is still relatively young compared to that of New Zealand and I really do not know whether I should be disheartened or should rejoice at the shorter life expectancy. A survey of the retirees in 2013 actually showed that only 2% of our retirees are financially independent—45% rely on family, 30% rely on charity, and 22% continue to work to be able to support themselves. I guess this stems from the misplaced reliance on pensions. Even within the Bangko Sentral or the Central Bank, we see the reliance on mandatory retirement in the choice of our workers. Our workers would rather withdraw the income from their funds, even if the pension is earning above-market rates. So instead of reinvesting it, they would rather withdraw it or they would rather maintain their mandatory deduction instead of opting to put in additional contributions.

Now we also see that our population is not aging, however. Fortunately, only 4% of our population is above 65 years old or above the retirement age and 52% of our population is still within the productive age, between 20 and 35. In light of this, we undertook the BSP Economic and Financial Learning Program (EFLP). The EFLP pushes for financial awareness and this serves different learning modules. Under the EFLP, we not only develop but also delivered innovative learning modules and tools, tailor-made to fit the participants' profile and proficiencies.

Just to give you an idea, we are quite fortunate that our unit handles both financial consumer protection and financial education, because our database on complaints has actually been a rich resource for developing our financial education modules. Emerging issues are identified early on and incorporated into our educational materials and learning programs.

So this just gives you the specific financial learning activities. We have expos, financial empowerment seminars, credit card awareness campaigns, and our new learning activity is AlertoAko. AlertoAko is actually an exhibit which features panels on frauds and scams—how to detect them, how to avoid them, what to do in case you fall victim to frauds and scams. We also have a specific exhibit for Money Matters for Kids, which is an interactive program for kids and we see that actually the adults accompanying the kids are enjoying this exhibit more than their children. So you can see that we have unintended beneficiaries from our exhibits.

We have also employed social media in our financial education initiatives and BSP now has an official Facebook and Twitter account. For all our learning activities, we conduct a knowledge-level survey before and after to check if there is an increase in knowledge and to check which points need to be emphasized. Our knowledge-level surveys actually show a remarkable increase in scores from pre- to post-test and we hope that we could soon also show that it changes how people think and behave.

We have also entered into strategic partnerships. Let me just give you some examples of these strategic partnerships we have with other government agencies. For the integration of financial lessons in the curriculum we work with the Department of Education. For our migrant workers, we cooperate with the Overseas Workers Welfare Administration, and for the base of the pyramid, we work with the Department of Social Welfare and Development. Also, as a member of the Financial Sector Forum, the financial regulators including the Insurance Commission and the Securities and Exchange Commission have come up with a "protect your money" campaign.

We have also adopted a financial consumer protection framework, which we believe will be a game changer for the Philippines. It incorporates an institutional analysis, financial consumer protection as an integral part of the business of banking and we have adopted the following principles—disclosure and transparency, fair treatment, protection of client information, effective recourse, and financial education.

For 2015, we look forward to rolling out the framework by launching a series of our road shows in targeted locations to show consumers what the framework could do for them. We will also develop an impact evaluation and monitoring tool to provide concrete evidence on our financial education initiatives. We have actually participated in the World Bank survey on financial capability of Filipinos, which will provide the baseline information for the development of our national financial inclusion strategy and also our national financial education strategy. So again, as we are developing our national financial inclusion strategy, we are grappling with the question of whether we should include financial education in the financial inclusion strategy or make a separate financial education strategy.

As a final note, we are aware that our success in financial education would not have been possible without the commitment of our BSP leadership and it has been a challenging but exciting journey for BSP. But I believe this is just the tip of the iceberg. We will continue to toil to finally make our dream of providing financial wellbeing for each and every Filipino a reality. Thank you very much.

Dr. Ganeshan Wignaraja: Thank you. Mr. Nguyen, please.

Evaluation of Financial Literacy in Viet Nam and National Financial Education Program

Nguyen Vinh Hung, Deputy Director General, International Cooperation Department, State Bank of Viet Nam: Good morning, ladies and gentlemen. I am delighted to give a presentation on financial literacy and financial education in Viet Nam. I would like to start off by saying something about our view of Viet Nam's financial sector. We have various types of financial institutions, but for the low-income, poor people, there are just three major financial institutions—the policy bank, the microfinance institution, and the state or commercial bank (Figure 4.5).

There have been no statistics so far, but we can say that financial services for low-income, poor people are provided largely by the informal financial sector. As you can see on the screen, the majority of our population lives in rural areas, with more than 60 million poor and low-income people, which accounts for 30% of the total population. As regards the small and the medium-sized enterprises (SMEs), 97% of them are SMEs and you can see the number of SMEs is growing every year.

Regarding financial literacy in Viet Nam, you can see our financial sector has developed in terms of its composition, the number of the financial institutions, and network coverage. Some financial institutions have the card network now at the community level. In conjunction with the increase in the quantity, quality, and diversification of financial services, there has also been an increase in the demand for financial services. Financial literacy in Viet Nam is not in line with the increase in the demand. The low level of financial literacy leads to wrong financial decisions. There are two kinds of wrong financial decision. There are those by people who are very conservative and keep their wealth in the form of cash or gold rather than putting their savings into formal financial institutions. Or there are those people who engage in high-risk financial activities but are not aware they are taking high risks.

The low financial literacy also makes it more difficult for people and enterprises to access formal financial services, so they have to rely on informal lenders and there are many negative consequences of borrowing from informal lenders. From the viewpoint of the financial institution, there is always a connection between the financial risk of the borrower and the credit risk of the financial institution.

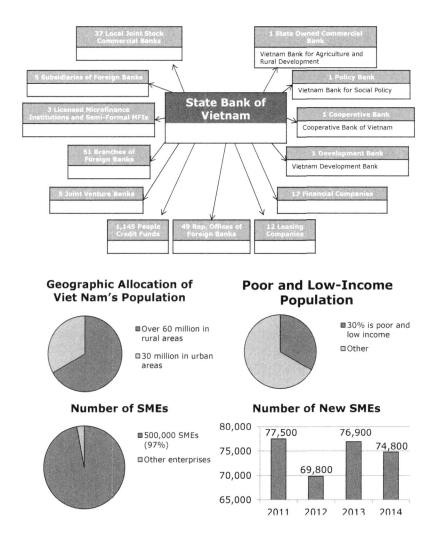

Figure 4.5   Overview of Viet Nam's financial sector
Source: Statistical database of the Banking Supervision Agency of the State Bank of Viet Nam.

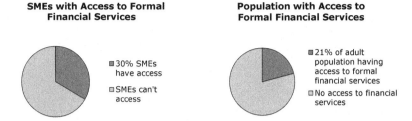

SMEs with Access to Formal Financial Services

- 30% SMEs have access
- SMEs can't access

Population with Access to Formal Financial Services

- 21% of adult population having access to formal financial services
- No access to financial services

- Overall access to and use of formal financial services is very low in Viet Nam compared with other countries in the region.
- Uneducated population segments have almost no access to financial services.
- The informal financial sector is probably the largest provider of financial services for low-income people, especially in rural areas.
- SMEs also have difficulty accessing formal financial services.

Figure 4.6   Access to formal financial services
Source: Statistical database of the Banking Supervision Agency of the State Bank of Vietnam.

As I mentioned earlier, there is a connection between financial literacy and access to formal financial services (Figure 4.6). You can see on the screen the overall access to and use of formal financial services is very low in Viet Nam compared with other countries in the region. Only 21% of the adult population have access to formal financial services and especially for the uneducated population segments access is more difficult. According to the World Bank's research, only 4.5% of people with primary school education or lower have a bank account with a formal institution.

Regarding informal financial services, as I mentioned, the informal financial sector is probably the largest provider of financial services to low-income people, especially in the rural and agricultural areas. As regards SMEs, they also have difficulties accessing formal financial services and only around 30% do in fact have access to formal financial services.

So why are financial institutions reluctant to provide access to their services? They worry about the repayment capacity of the borrower as they do not have transparent information about the financial situation of the borrower. They also have concerns about the capacity of the borrower to manage the business effectively and safely. When lending to rural and agricultural areas, loans are usually small and administration costs are high in remote areas, so banks have to think twice if they want to invest in the necessary technology. There are also deficiencies of the operational networks of financial institution. Finally, poor and low-income people usually do not have the collateral needed to borrow money.

From the viewpoint of households or SMEs, their low financial literacy makes it difficult to manage their potential risks or make good financial decisions. It also is difficult for them to prove to the banks they have the capacity of financial management and repayment. Also, they do not have collateral. As I mentioned earlier, use of informal financial services can have many negative consequences, such as becoming the victim of fraud and incurring huge losses.

Let me give one example of a financial literacy issue in consumer credit. As you know, consumer credit is an important method of purchasing goods and it is increasingly being demanded in Viet Nam, especially by the young and the middle-income segments of the population. Consumer credit is offered by some banks and financial companies, but its operation is still new and the financial literacy about consumer credit is still limited. Homecredit is a very famous financial company in Viet Nam, offering consumer credit. In 2013, it conducted a survey of 1,000 people visiting a shopping center in an urban area. They found that only 51% of people had good knowledge of consumer credit, 42% had limited knowledge, and 7% had no idea about consumer credit. Please note that those surveyed were middle-income people as they were interviewed at a shopping center in an urban area. We can assume they were educated people and that their income is quite good; they were not poor, low-income people.

Another example is a survey of the Department of Education and Training in Ho Chi Minh City, which is the commercial center of Viet Nam. They conducted a survey in seven high schools over two years, before and after the financial education program (Figure 4.7). I will not go into the details of the survey, but after the education program, the number of children who have knowledge about financial matters and money management had increased.

What is the current situation of financial education in Viet Nam? Most SMEs and households do not have appropriate financial education and financial education in schools is mostly directed at a certain groups of students and mostly concerned with academic topics, not knowledge

· Survey of Department of Education and Training of Ho Chi Minh City at 7 high
  schools in 2012 and 2013 on money management of children aged 13 to 18.

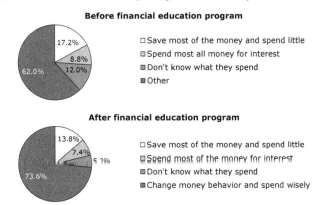

Before financial education program

☐ Save most of the money and spend little
☐ Spend most all money for interest
▨ Don't know what they spend
▨ Other

After financial education program

☐ Save most of the money and spend little
▨ Spend most of the money for interest
▨ Don't know what they spend
▨ Change money behavior and spend wisely

Figure 4.7   Example of financial literacy: money management behavior of children
Source: Statistical database of the Banking Supervision Agency of the State Bank of
Vietnam.

useful for everyday life regarding financial management, such as cash
management, saving, and insurance. So far, there has not been a national
financial education program policy, so this makes Viet Nam different
from other countries.

Box 4.1 shows some examples of financial education programs
offered by some financial institutions in Viet Nam. The national financial
education program—as I mentioned, because there has been no national
program so far, there is no agency that has a mandate to establish such
a program, so it is just my suggestion to have a national program in
Viet Nam. So the drawback of current financial education programs
is that they are small, targeted at only certain groups, and biased by
the interests of the provider. For example, financing companies offer
education programs on consumer credit, but I think it is only to promote
their services. That is why we need a national financial program.

However, in order to have a national program, there are some
challenges. This education needs to be facilitated by government
regulation and it needs to have the involvement of credible entities. One
difficulty is how to assess the needs of financial education of various
groups of people and SMEs. We need to establish the national financial
education strategy with the two targets of protecting customers and

Box 4.1   Financial education in Viet Nam

Vietnam Bank for Social Policies

Financial education program started in 2007 and financed by Citi Foundation. The program is for borrowers of the bank, who are the poor in Ha Noi and neighboring provinces.

HSBC Vietnam

In 2012, HSBC Vietnam initiated a financial education program, including an online library of financial education with 10 modules (personal finance and enterprise finance) and a pilot training program in elementary schools, namely "Junior Achievement More than Money.™"

Home Credit

The program started in 2013 in cooperation with large shopping centers. This is a financial knowledge consultation program "Think it through, sign it wisely." The program is for consumer credit.

Visa International

The program started in 2013 in cooperation with the Central Student Association of Vietnam. The program's purpose is to provide education on financial literacy for students in universities.

Save the Children International and Citi Foundation

The Financial Education Project for secondary schools is in cooperation with the Department of Education and Training. The project has been implemented in 100 Secondary Schools in Ho Chi Minh City, with more than 3,000 pupils and 300 parents benefiting directly from the project.

Aflatoun Program for Children

In cooperation with the Hue City People Committee and Vietnam Association for the Protection of Children's Rights (VAPCR), this is a financial education program for children from 6 to 14 years of age.

Source: State Bank of Vietnam.

improving financial literacy. There are also the challenges of establishing cooperation among relevant agencies for the program, and of finding the resources necessary to implement the national program.

Box 4.2 lists what I think are the requirements for the national financial education program. The program needs to provide common guidance and standards for specific financial education programs. The program should cover a wide range of locations and beneficiaries. The program should be continuous—it should not be a one-time effort. It

Box 4.2   National financial education program: Requirements

- Provide common guidance or standards for specific financial education programs, ensure them practically.
- Cover a wide range of locations and beneficiaries.
- Be continuous.
- Follow a national strategy.
- Promote the involvement of various parties in the program as well as the principles of sharing responsibilities, efficiency, and expansion of good models.
- Develop action plan for the program and establish a roadmap with milestones within a timeframe.

Source: Author.

Box 4.3   Phasing of national financial education program

Phase 1: Financial education for the poor, low-income, and women in rural areas and SMEs
- Specify a national coordinating agency for the program.
- Develop a national financial education program.
- Develop a set of basic standard modules for financial education as a platform for specific training programs.
- Develop the capacity of human resources and physical resources for financial education.
- Recommend amendment or establishment of new government policies and regulations to support the national program.

Phase 2: General financial education for all groups of population via the formal education system.
- Incorporate financial education as formal units in the curriculums of schools (from elementary to high schools) and universities.
- Establish financial education training centers or financial education supporting centers for various demands.
- Require and establish financial education services for clients at banks, financial companies, and other financial institutions.

Source: Author.

should follow a national strategy and it should promote the involvement of various parties in the program, especially the private sector. An action plan should be developed for the program, with a concrete roadmap and milestones.

So in my opinion, we need a coordinating agency for a national program to coordinate all efforts (see Box 4.3). Such an agency needs to have adequate resources and the authority to coordinate various entities. These are my suggestions for phasing in a national financial education program in Viet Nam. The first phase would be for the current situation and the second phase would be after financial education is introduced into the formal education system. That is the end of my presentation. Thank you for your attention.

Dr. Ganeshan Wignaraja: Thank you very much. We will go straight to you, Ms. Kosolwongse.

Promoting Access to Capital Markets by the SEC Thailand

Nichaya Kosolwongse, Visiting Fellow, Asian Financial Partnership Center, FSA: Ladies and gentlemen, good morning. My name is Nichaya. I come from the Thai Securities and Exchange Commission (SEC), but now I am a visiting fellow under the Asian Financial Partnership Center (AFPAC) program. I have been training with the Financial Services Agency of Japan (FSA) for almost for four months. In my presentation today, I will cover how SEC Thailand promotes access to capital markets.

This is very important because promoting access to capital markets is the first step to the development of capital markets in Thailand. This has two dimensions. The first dimension is the investor side, where we have the financial literacy outreach program. The other dimension is the issuer side, which encompasses two of our projects—the IPO Pride of the Provinces project (IPOP for short) and the SME bonds.

So let me start with the investor side first. This is the financial literacy outreach program. We divide it into two parts. The first one is about basic financial knowledge and the other one is about investment knowledge. We also have different target groups and different objectives. For the financial knowledge part, the key message is how to earn, save, and grow money, whereas for the investment knowledge part our key message is that investment is necessary for everyone and we should make investments that suit our risk profiles based on sufficient information.

Among our executed strategies here, first we are doing a cost-effectiveness assessment through various channels. We have new media, mass media, face-to-face activities, and also the language must be plain and understandable, and it is not just education, but it is also entertainment. We use the same content for different channels and, lastly, we also use networking.

For the first one, the new media. We launched a website for investor education, start-to-invest.com, in 2012. Before that, investor education was part of the Thai SEC website, but now we separate it. At the same time, we have a mobile phone application, which we call start-to-invest also. This is for the young generation and we think that it helps them to learn financial planning; they can set the goals and choose what they would like to invest in.

In terms of mass media, we used many channels. For example, we published articles in business newspapers. We have advertisements in lifestyle magazines. These show celebrities giving money tips—famous stars, famous actors, actresses, and so on. We also have publications to distribute to investors during exhibitions.

For TV programs, we have a one-minute scoop, Start-to-invest, in an English teaching program, Chris Delivery. This is quite a famous show in Thailand. And for movies, we have also a message tied in with the movie named Super Salaryman. The theme is "manage your life, manage your money." We also have a sitcom and a Thai folk song on television. For radio, we have a short radio program called One Minute for a Better Life with the SEC during the mid-day national news program, and for cartoons we have one called Malaeng-Mao Investor.

In terms of face-to-face activities, we have a talk show, which features a famous comedian, who shares some of her money management experience with the audience. And every year we have theme booths in exhibitions held in the city and at the money expo.

We have an upcoming event, a reality show called The Money. This is the first financial reality show ever in Thailand. We will select 12 participants from a nationwide audition who will compete for a prize of 1 million baht. This will concentrate on personal finance, debt management, savings, and investment.

We received an award from the Stock Exchange of Thailand (SET) for the city exhibition, money expo, and mobile application. Apart from what I talked about, we are planning some other projects. One big project is Finance in the Workplace. This is meant to promote employees' financial literacy and skills through programs organized by employers, with the human resources unit playing a key role along with the financial advocate. They will be trained as financial instructors and will focus on knowledge transfer or activities in their organization. In fact, 168 organizations and companies have already joined and assigned representatives to attend the training courses so far.

Another project is called "A Thousand Baht, Start a Journey to Your Dream." This is meant to promote investment and saving discipline among the working-age population. Investors can invest in participated mutual funds at a minimum of 1,000 baht every month to achieve their medium- and long-term goals for retirement.

For the issuers side, as I said, we have two projects. The first one is the IPOP. This is to encourage potential companies in the countryside to raise funds in the stock market and we provide some privileges. So we have the qualification of the participants, the benefits they can get is that they are able to attend the training courses on capital markets, fundraising, and preparations for becoming a listed company, and they can seek advice for the initial public offering (IPO) from the financial advisors, auditors, the SET, and also the Thai SEC. They will also be granted an exemption from the application fee for the IPO by the SEC and the SET. If they can obtain approval for the IPO within the deadline, they will be awarded a plate of honor. Up to now, 290 companies from the 39 provinces have participated, 27 of which, accounting for 10%, are already listed on our Stock Exchange.

For the SME bonds, we have the same concept as the IPOP. The purpose here is to facilitate fundraising for SMEs through the bond market with certain benefits. The scope of the program is that it will cover only plain bonds and bills, which will be offered to the board of professional investors and retail investors. To qualify, participants must be companies with net assets not exceeding 2 billion baht. The benefits they can obtain for joining the program are participation in the training courses to acquire a background in capital markets and education on the rules and regulations relating to bond issuance.

They can have their application fees for bond issuance approval waived and get a discount on the submission fee for the initial filing registration from the Thai SEC. Lastly, they can apply for a rating bond with a credit rating agency at a lower cost. Up to now, 97 companies have participated in this program, 57% of which are non-listed. So far, we have seen an increase in demand for the SME bonds from the accredited investor funds.

Okay, that is my presentation. Thank you so much.

Open Floor Discussion

Dr. Ganeshan Wignaraja: Thank you, Ms. Kosolwongse. Now we will open up the session for questions for about 20 minutes. I propose to handle this time in the following way. I will pose a question to each of the panelists, but please do not answer straight away. We will then open it up to the floor and collect all the questions, and give you a couple of minutes to answer. How efficiently we do this will depend on your cooperation from the floor. Please ask your question clearly and address it to a particular panelist.

So let me start with a question to Dr. Hadad. Could you highlight one or two key lessons from the experience of developing the national literacy strategy for Indonesia, with a diverse geography of 20,000 islands? What are the main takeaways?

To Dr. Ahmed, it is striking that Pakistan has a population of 188 million characterized by a high level of financial exclusion. Since you have limited resources, would you target particular groups or would you go for a more functional approach?

To Attorney Kasala, how do you best target financial education for an important vulnerable group such as gender in the Philippines? Then within that, would you target young women separately from seniors?

For Mr. Nguyen, it seems that Viet Nam just started its financial education strategy and the informal sector is the main provider, which sometimes has challenges. What are the next steps for implementing Viet Nam's vision for financial education?

To Ms. Kosolwongse, Thailand has a plethora of programs for financial education. Which is the most effective and what indicators can we really seriously use to measure success or is it merely a public relations campaign?

Professor Yoshino, please.

Naoyuki Yoshino, Dean, ADBI and Chief Advisor, FSA Institute: Okay, thank you very much for all the presentations. I would like to ask about mobile banking in the Asian region. I think accepting deposits by mobile banking may be good. However, making loans may be slightly different because they have to look at the customers. So I wonder, do you need a kind of diversified financial system, one for accepting deposits and one for the lending side? Also, in Indonesia and Myanmar, we are proposing using post office networks. So Muliaman Hadad, what would be your frank opinion about utilizing those facilities, especially on the many islands and in the many rural areas you have? Thank you very much.

Dr. Ganeshan Wignaraja: Thank you. Prof. Fornero, please.

Elsa Fornero, Professor, University of Turin and Center for Research on Pensions and Welfare Policies: Okay, I have a question for Mr. Ahmed. I was particularly struck by your figures. You said 56% of your population does not have any access to financial services. I wonder whether you have a compulsory pension system, because if you have a compulsory pension system it means that people are required to pay contributions and that is a form of saving. So they could be reached somehow through the pension system and it could be a factor that somehow makes inclusion easier.

Dr. Ganeshan Wignaraja: Thank you very much. Ms. Lewis, please?

Sue Lewis, Chair, UK Financial Services Consumer Panel: Yes, thank you. I have a question about how keen people are to learn about financial matters. It is a question for everybody, really. I mean if you tried to run financial education programs in the United Kingdom, you would not get very far because people really do not want to learn, so I am interested to know if there are lessons from developing economies where people actually are keen to learn about financial matters. I also have a question about Thailand. To what extent does your sort of trying to get people to invest go hand in hand with appropriate consumer protection? Because when you are trying to build your market, you also need to protect consumers. I just wondered how that worked. Sorry, two questions, thank you.

Dr. Ganeshan Wignaraja: Is there someone at the back?

Audience member: Two things. The government agencies have been very kind to portray that they have been doing a lot of things in financial education, but I would like to share some of the experience working in financial education in the field, particularly in Pakistan and the Philippines, another Asian country, with a huge number of migrant workers. Is there any special pilot program for migrant workers on financial education? That looks to be very key.

The second one is the informal sector. When we talk about the compulsory pension and everything, when there is a very huge informal sector, that looks almost impossible. In the training of SMEs, the main prohibitively difficult part seems to be the huge paperwork for the SMEs to get the loans. Has there been any experience among the countries to share with us? So I am just curious about it. Thank you.

Dr. Ganeshan Wignaraja: Thank you very much. We have time for one last question and then we shall turn it over to the panel.

Audience member: Basically, we are talking about a large rural population. They remain in the unorganized sector. Somebody mentioned migrant workers. Besides migrant workers, there are many who are not in the formal sector. So what kind of strategies are needed, because there is a large number to be reached? One needs to talk about campaigning, but to achieve a certain level of literacy focused inputs are required. So what kind of strategies have been thought about in, for example, Indonesia, Pakistan, and other Asian countries? It is a straight question.

Dr. Ganeshan Wignaraja: Thank you very much. Dr. Hadad, would you like to respond to some points?

Dr. Muliaman D. Hadad: Thank you very much for the question, Mr. Chair. Very important lesson learned, well at least for Indonesia. Indonesia has for quite some time been dealing with the issues surrounding microfinance. I think for the last 40 years, governments and other parts of the country or related parties in the country are very much focused on microfinance, but the poverty level is still quite significant. Financial literacy and also inequality are still quite a concern.

The question is what went wrong with this? Perhaps it is not only an issue of Indonesia. Everyone or every country is dealing with microfinance, but inequality of access to finance is still very much the issue. The question is what went wrong? That is why the very important lesson learned is that microfinance is only halfway. Then the rest of the way is basically how to improve inclusion. That is why it is very important to shift the paradigm from microfinance to financial inclusion. This shifting paradigm is very important because microfinance is just one side of the coin, and the other side of the coin is very much about empowerment, opening access, regulation, technology, and so on and so forth. This is why we need to come up with a national strategy.

Our national strategy is basically to equip our infrastructure with microfinance and then to fill in the other side of the gap. That is the basic lesson we have learned for the last 40 years when dealing with microfinance, but then the issue is still access. That is why to fill the gap we come up with a national strategy, we have to move from microfinance to financial inclusion. That perhaps is very much the important lesson learned.

Then the second question from Professor Yoshino on mobile banking. Indonesia has just launched what we call branchless banking, also accompanied by what we call digital payment facilities. In our branchless banking, we hire a lot of agents in the very remote areas. Then the agent is under supervision of the banks, the related banks. So the bank's closest branches are responsible for supervising agents.

What can be done by agents? Agents can be a point where people can not only keep a basic savings account, but the agent on behalf of the bank can also provide access to loans. So the branchless banking that we offer is basically aimed at scaling down banking services at the agent level. A banking service then is not only about saving, but lending issues too can be handled at the agent level. Of course there is a limit to what can be provided at the agent level, but at least access to finance will be significantly improved compared with the use of informal lenders. Actually, we have already started and the early indicators suggest that there will be some very important results on this.

The last one from Professor Yoshino on postal banking. I just visited one of the postal banks here in Tokyo yesterday. It is very interesting and we are going to go in that direction, but there is a long way to go because we have to change the rules and regulations. In particular, the rules governing our postal office because our postal office is very much focused on postal activities. The postal office had been dealing with financial issues but as banking expanded quite significantly, the postal office reduced its role in the financial business. To improve access to finance, I think it is good to empower our postal services, so they not only engage in postal services as a business, but also engage in banking, insurance, and so on and so forth. Because microinsurance is also very important for the people in the area.

That is it, I think, for the questions directed to me. Thank you.

Dr. Ganeshan Wignaraja: Thank you. Dr. Ahmed, please.

Dr. Saeed Ahmed: Thank you. First let me answer your question, Dr. Wignaraja. Your question was in a population of about 188 million, we have a high level of financial exclusion—are we pursuing a target group segmentation approach to promote financial literacy or are we pursuing a more functional approach? The straight answer is we are pursuing a more functional approach. The reason is that we did a baseline survey prior to launching the financial literacy program and we found that 40% of the unbanked population did not have access because they were not aware of the financial products and services. So financial literacy was a major barrier.

So we launched a program and our focus was initially on the low-income sector, which was the unbanked population. Because financial inclusion is a broader challenge in Pakistan, it is not a gender issue, it is not confined to any specific regions or any particular groups. We pursued a more functional approach to design a financial literacy program, but of course the program's content was developed to suit the context of the clients, particularly the low-income people. Most of them are functionally illiterate because the literacy level is low in Pakistan as well.

Having said that, there is no one-size-fits-all strategy, which was this more functional approach, because we thought that the level of financial exclusion is high so we need to target the unbanked, low-income population. Given that, if you look at the demographic profile of Pakistan, two-thirds of the population lives in the rural areas, but if you look at the financial access, one-third of the rural population has financial access. So that is a geographic mismatch. If you choose to pursue a target group when adopting a segmentation approach, then perhaps you could design programs which are both targeted at the rural population and also at women. We saw that the level of financial exclusion among women is higher than for men. So you could design specific programs for men and for women.

Most importantly, I showed in my presentation the demographic profile of Pakistan, that out of 188 million people, over 100 million are below the age of 25. So the children and youth component for financial literacy programs becomes very important. We did not have a children and youth component in the initial pilot phase, but going forward in the national rollout we are going to have a separate component for targeting children and youth, because we feel that it is very important to develop financial capability among the future generations. So that is my answer to your question.

Let me add to the answer from my Indonesian colleague on mobile banking—that mobile banking is mobilizing deposits, but what about the loans? I think if you look at the evolution of mobile banking in the Philippines, Kenya, Pakistan, Indonesia, and other countries, you will see that in the first stage of development of mobile banking, there is more emphasis on over-the-counter transactions. So the people use branchless banking for domestic remittances or utility bill payments or government-to-person (G2P) payment transfers.

As branchless banking develops, you see more uptake of mobile wallets, that is deposit accounts. But how to use mobile banking channels for loans? I think it is easier. What we have seen in Pakistan is that microfinance banks are now doing loan application appraisals at their branches, but once a loan has been approved after due diligence of clients, the money can be disbursed through branchless banking channels. The unregulated microfinance institutions which are not branchless banking providers develop partnerships with the branchless banking providers to collect the repayment of the microfinance loans.

So repayment of microfinance loans is already happening in Pakistan. I think at the next stage we see that the agents have the capacity to do loan application appraisals. So then the loan application approval and disbursement can be done at the agents' location. At the moment, it is merely being used for repayment of microfinance loans.

To answer the question of Professor Fornero, the straight answer is no, we do not have any compulsory pension plan. We do have a 56% financially excluded population and the main reasons for financial exclusion are the lack of financial access and financial literacy, because the population is unaware of the financial products and services, so they cannot access them. So access to appropriate financial products and services that meet their demand is one reason for the low level of financial literacy. And also, if you look at the demographic profile, over 50% of Pakistan's population, nearly 60%, is below the poverty line, if you take $2 a day as the definition for the poverty line.

So with 60% of the population below the poverty line, which are economically inactive, you cannot have any compulsory pension schemes. But we do have compulsory pension schemes for those working for the government or in the industrial sectors. For the ultra-poor, for the poorest of the poor, the government does have social safety net programs that provide direct cash grants to the needy people.

Dr. Ganeshan Wignaraja: Thank you. Attorney Kasala, please.

Ms. Atty. Prudence Angelita A. Kasala: As regards gender-specific training modules, the Philippines does not yet have gender-specific training. However, we do recognize and we are in the process of actually developing gender-specific training in recognition of the role of women, especially in handling finances. As you know, in the Philippines women actually hold the purse in the family, so men work and they give their salaries to their wives. We envision that the workshops for women would be more interactive, would have more practical exercises on budgeting and planning.

Do we see any difference in addressing young women and old women? Yes. We see that there would be a difference in delivery mechanisms, especially for older women who prefer face-to-face contact. As regards the other questions propounded by Ms. Lewis, how keen are people to get financial education? Actually, the uptake is very low, so we really have to give them incentives. When we engage in face-to-face contact, we do a lot of contests and games so that people will be enticed to participate and to learn. So we do spend a substantial amount of money or budget for our financial education initiatives.

On the migrant workers, I think we should train not only the workers themselves, but also their beneficiaries, because the migrant workers actually send a lot of their earnings to their beneficiaries and we see a lot of beneficiaries just spending left and right when they receive the money. So one of our measurements also is to look at the disposition of the remittances by the beneficiaries.

On microfinance or extension of loans to microenterprises, we have also implemented tiered "know your customer" (KYC) requirements. Knowing that microentrepreneurs have fewer documents to deal with, we also impose proportionate documentation requirements on these entities. Thank you.

Mr. Nguyen Vinh Hung: In regard to the next step, to implement national financial education in Viet Nam, I think at the moment we have various financial education programs offered by various entities, but we have not got any national strategy or national program for financial education. So I think the first step is to encourage and facilitate our current programs offered by various entities and the government needs to regulate that operation, but regulate in a good way. Not to control them, but to increase the good practice.

There are various ways to encourage financial institutions and other entities to offer financial education programs. For example, from the viewpoint of the central bank, we regulate the banks so we can offer them tax exemption for the expenses of the financial institution when they conduct the financial education program. The next step is to set up a national coordinating agency for the national program. The first is to develop the program itself and the second to implement and to supervise the implementation of the national program. Also that agency needs to ensure all targets of the national program are achieved.

Regarding the question on the post office, in Viet Nam we have one bank called Lien Viet Bank. Last year, they bought the post system of Viet Nam, so now they are the only bank that owns the post office system for the whole country. However, at the moment the post office can only provide cash services like money transfer or receiving savings; they cannot provide loans to people. The reason is that the banks have to consider the costs and benefits. The number of credit officers they would need for the whole post system would be too high, according to the CEO of the bank regarding such activities.

As regards your question about how keen people are to receive financial education, yes, I agree with my colleagues from the Philippines. When they have an incentive and the incentive is that they have to use financial services, that is where the government should step in to raise awareness, to educate people about why it is necessary to learn financial knowledge. By doing so, the government can support the efforts of other entities who are providing the financial education at the moment. Thank you.

Dr. Ganeshan Wignaraja: Thank you very much. Ms. Kosolwongse, please.

Ms. Nichaya Kosolwongse: Regarding your question, where we have been most effective so far, our main achievement so far, is financial literacy in the workplace, because we got a good response from the participating organizations. The tool for the measurement of impact of the program is that we request for them to report to the Thai SEC twice a year, and they have to consult with us for the method that they use for their measurement. For example they must have the evaluation form for their staff. If they want to boost the saving accounts for the staff in the organization, they have to show the bank account statement and we will say that, okay, the number of the deposit accounts increased.

Another one, on the issuer side, we have the IPOP, IPO Pride of the Provinces project. This one is quite an achievement, also because we can see that the percentage of companies that have been listed on the stock market is okay, I think—good enough, 10% so far.

Back to the question of Ms. Lewis on consumer protection. Yes, we think that it is important. We realize it and we are concerned about consumer protection, so having at first focused on investor education, we now move to consumer protection at the point of sale. Because we think that actually the investor is most in need of it at the point of sale, when they have to make an investment decision. So we have proposed a knowledge test for some more complicated products to inform the investor about what question to ask and what they need to know, the key product-specific risks. They have to answer the test, and if they get the wrong answer, they have to read the solution and learn more, and they have to sign that they acknowledge the specific risk of such complex products.

Dr. Ganeshan Wignaraja: Thank you very much. The big message from this session is that financial education does matter for Asian economies. It also influences financial inclusion and the effective regulation of various actors. The main lessons can be viewed under three basic headings.

The first lesson is that we have got to do the diagnostics and surveys are really important tools. There are different kinds of surveys. We have access to finance surveys, consumer finance surveys, and financial literacy surveys. So we have a very heterogeneous survey experience in the room, but what really comes out is that we have got to use international standard methodologies for surveys, so we can benchmark across countries to see where Asian countries stand over time. Benchmarking and trying to understand better the reality enables effective strategy development.

The second lesson concerns national strategy, which is vital for dealing with the challenges faced by Asian economies. I have four sub-points under this heading:

    a.   We have got to have coordination among the different stakeholders—government, the education sector, financial institutions, and, very important, civil society. They should be involved in strategy development and implementation.

b. The customer is king. I think a colleague said that, but we have also got to look at both the demand and the supply sides.

c. We usually rely on functional approaches because resources are limited. But, we can, and particularly over time as income rises and the effectiveness is proven, target the most vulnerable groups, be it gender, be it youth, or be it the seniors.

d. Use technology. I was fascinated by the Thai presentation emphasizing mobile banking and many different programs for the young. Then for the old, we have got to think about other ways of teaching. So I think technology use comes under national strategies, and it is important to learn from good international practice.

The final lesson really concerns implementation of strategy and the key point is about the monitoring and evaluation, which is vital for lesson learning and adaptation of strategy. I was struck by Dr. Hadad's interesting point about microfinance. Microfinance is touted as the solution for inclusion, but does it really work, and if so, can it go to scale? Banks dominate the financial sectors of Asian economies, and can usefully complement smaller microfinance initiatives rather than crowd them out. So we have got to do a lot of monitoring and evaluation but it is very difficult to do, it is expensive and the incentives may not be there. So the only extra point I want to add is maybe because ADBI is a think tank, you have also got to use think tanks in your countries as a tool, to try to help with the monitoring and evaluation, you have got to provide the incentives.

We have had a fascinating session and I would like everyone to give a big hand to our panel. Thank you so much.

Session 5

Wrap-Up

Naoyuki Yoshino, Dean, ADBI and Chief Advisor, FSA Institute: Thank you very much. This is the final wrap-up session and we are planning to talk about all the summaries of today's discussion. We have four panelists. The first one is Director Satoshi Saito from the Bank of Japan. The Bank of Japan has set up many financial business education systems. At first the Bank of Japan started promotion of household savings, that was in the 1960s I think, then they moved into much wider financial education. The second commentator is Flore-Anne Messy. She has been working on financial education for many years and has visited many countries, so she has a lot of knowledge about this area. The third panelist is Miles Larbey, who has been appearing in many sessions in the past two days. The last one is Mr. Nguyen from Viet Nam.

I think Europe, the United States, New Zealand, and Asian countries have slightly different levels of financial education. So I would like to start with Mr. Saito for some comments on the Japanese experience.

Satoshi Saito, Director, Head of Financial Services Information Division, Public Relations Department, Bank of Japan: Thank you for your introduction. It is my very great honor to participate in this symposium as a panelist and I would like to thank the staff of ADBI, OECD, FSA, and all involved. In this symposium, there are three important points, I think. The first point is the increasing importance of life planning. In each country, life planning is the first step in a series of actions to be taken by each individual toward financial independence and a better life. The longer the retirement period is in an aging population, the more significant a life plan is.

In Japan, financial education for adults tended to concentrate on providing accurate and fair information on various financial products, but now we are changing that slightly. With this change, we have to focus on the people who are not interested in life planning at all, but who are most in need of such education. Now our problem is how to provide them with the necessary information and how to encourage them to take appropriate actions. Honestly, we have not found an effective solution yet, but yesterday's session suggests that using insights from behavioral economics and consumer psychology might be very helpful.

In Japan, we recommend installment savings plans, which are automatically and regularly deducted from salary payments. I think this is one effective practice. In addition, the session suggests some effective ways to approach such people. We are still trying to distribute the brochure, but visual materials and storytelling, very interesting to me, may be more effective.

The second point is the necessity of developing a framework for financial education in schools. To do so, we have to cooperate much more closely with the Ministry of Education. Financial education in school plays a very important role in establishing the foundation for financial literacy in terms of knowledge and attitudes. In school, we have to teach the importance of life planning, the concept of scarcity of money and resources, and basic knowledge of financial literacy such as interest, inflation, deflation, risk, and return. At the national level, we have to make efforts to include financial education in the national education curriculum to secure enough lesson time within several subjects such as mathematics, civics, and home economics. Especially in Japan, we spend very few hours teaching financial education.

At the same time, we have to develop a system for training and supporting teachers who are not well trained. In Japan, some financial industry groups hold seminars for teachers. We have to try to increase such seminars and to support teachers. Financial industry groups can dispatch retirees who can teach financial knowledge gained in financial institutions and provide materials including visual materials. In cooperation with schools, we have to make the best use of such resources.

The third point is the potential of digital tools. From experience, we know that visual materials are more effective than written materials. How about digital tools? Webpages are very convenient. We do not have to print or distribute books and revise them. For users, it is also convenient. They can access pages from anywhere and the information provided is always up to date. However, I think there are more effective ways to use them, for example, the online tools of the Australian Securities and Investments Commission presented yesterday. In Japan, we also provide a simulator for life planning on our webpage, which links to the page of the national pension authority. Many people use this simulator.

Everyone knows how complex and troublesome it is to simulate one's financial life plan—many people find it troublesome, many people cannot do that. If online tools can support their decision making, it is very helpful. I think such use of digital tools is one of the challenges of the future.

In the previous sessions, I heard that the OECD is preparing a paper on digital tools. Is that correct? If so, I am very much looking forward to the publication of that study. Thank you for your kindness.

Dean Naoyuki Yoshino: Thank you very much. Our next panelist is Flore-Anne Messy.

Flore-Anne Messy, Deputy Head, Financial Affairs Division, OECD and Executive Secretary of OECD/INFE: Thank you, Dean Yoshino. I prepared a few slides but do not worry, it will not be a 20-slide presentation. First, I think, the good news—and I believe all of you are already convinced—is that financial education can work, but only under certain conditions. Of course, we discussed a lot of them yesterday and this morning. The first condition is evidence. As was mentioned in this morning's session, evidence can come from different surveys and the main purpose is to identify the financial literacy, or I should also say, inclusion needs, but also the context in which individuals are living and the responsibilities, the risks they have to address in their life are really important. Of course, this can vary from country to country, but also from household to household, or from individual to individual. So it is very important to really understand the consumers and the households well in order to develop financial education.

The second condition is an enabling environment and a framework and this is a national strategy for financial education. Of course, the OECD is a big promoter of that, so I do not need to explain a lot about this, but I think what is really key within this framework is coordination and partnership; these are two words, it may look very simple. I know that in practice it can be challenging. So this is something that should not be overlooked and this is something that is often built up over time in countries.

The third is the importance of clear and agreed objectives. I would like to add that, to have a good national strategy, the objective needs to be measureable, so it can be evaluated and adapted to the national context. As was said in the previous sessions, there is no one-size-fits-all model for national strategy. It really needs to fit the national context. And of course if we are speaking about pensions, for example, it should really take into account the pension system and its characteristics.

Starting early is also very important. We have talked a lot about schools. I would like to say that what is really important is to start as early as possible. In some countries, I know that there are a lot of children outside of school. These children should not be left out. What is really important is that financial education habits and behavior are nurtured at a very early stage, so that every individual has the building blocks of what planning ahead means, enabling them to differentiate between needs and wants.

First, of course, we need the schools. In addition to having financial education in schools, as was mentioned by my colleague from the Bank of Japan, we also need supporting tools in order for this to work. It is not enough to have financial education in the curriculum. It is a good thing, but I know in many countries they just say, let us have financial education as a mandatory topic in our curriculum. That is all nice, and from an OECD perspective we welcome that. But I know that if the resources are not there to train the teachers, to develop pedagogical tools, this is simply not working and can even be detrimental, because although officially there is financial education in schools, there is no impact on students. Some may conclude, therefore, that financial education is not working, when actually nothing is happening because there is no support for teachers and there is no support for students. So it is very important to have the right support for teachers, students, and also for parents for this to work well.

Second, we need to design, implement, and of course evaluate any kinds of initiatives based on consumers' biases and preferences. We talked a lot about behavioral biases, procrastination, consumers being inactive and not being able to take decisions. We need to build on these characteristics to develop financial education programs that are effective. One of the good ways is to make it interactive and a lot of the speakers have been mentioning that storytelling and visualization are also very important. So let us build on the things that we know are working.

I also want to stress that, of course, when we were looking into this subject within the International Network on Financial Education (INFE), we were considering whether we should focus on knowledge, attitude, or behavior. Now much research has been done. We know that knowledge is part of the picture, but it is not enough. We really need to develop the skills, the habits, and I would like to say the attitudes. Motivation is extremely important—extremely important for people, first, to participate in financial education programs and, second, to act upon them. This can be done in many ways, but I think building on community effect, peer effect, is really important. Social media can also play an important role.

I wanted to end with sustainability. We discussed this especially yesterday—it was Ms. Lewis who raised it—and I think it is especially important. We really have momentum for financial education and I heard all of us in the room want to do as much as we can now, but for this to work for future generations, we need the long term and for that we need the resources. We also need institutions that are independent and can continue the work. So when I am hearing for example Viet Nam saying, we are considering having an independent body that can do financial education, I would say, yes, that is very good practice, but I would say also that in addition to being independent and having the resources, you need credibility. So this is also kind of a process—to be credible for the population, for other institutions that are around you, for the government. This is also something that is built over time.

Second, I said yesterday I do not want to be naïve about financial education. I am not trying to sell you the silver bullet that is going to solve

188 Promoting Better Lifetime Planning through Financial Education

all of our problems. No, I do not believe that. I think financial education is very useful, but not a panacea. First, we know it is a long-term process and the objective is not only to change behavior, as I said yesterday. It is really to improve financial wellbeing and I think everybody should keep that in mind. Focusing on behavior, we may think we want all of our consumers to save. Well yes, saving is a good thing but if you are overly indebted, the first thing you might have to do is just repay your debt. So policymakers do not know it all and individuals, well, we are doing financial education to equip them with the competency to decide for themselves and choose the course of action that is the most rational in their situation.

They should be the ones that know best about their situation. Regarding focusing on financial wellbeing, I will say a bit about what we are trying to do at the OECD on this. Policymakers quite often want to see short-term outcomes. Maybe some of you in the room are faced with this kind of challenge. My boss, my government, they want to see the result tomorrow and not in 10 or 20 years' time. For short-term outcomes, I would like to say that financial education is maybe not the best course of action. You may prefer default options; you may prefer regulation. That is fine, but know that these are not silver bullets either. They have drawbacks.

With that, you are not equipping financial consumers with the competencies to face change in the future, because we are living in a world that is changing so fast that we need individuals not only to behave the way we want, but also to be able to adapt to change, even faster than regulation. So yes, you can use regulation, but I strongly believe, and we strongly believe at the OECD, it will not be enough.

What we propose instead is to have financial education in association with the default mechanisms, regulatory measures, just because we know financial education takes some time and that with the serious risks or very important responsibilities the consumer now has, it may be useful to have default options or regulation. It is typically the case for pensions and can be typically the case for catastrophic risk. We did not discuss this so much, but of course making sure that people have insurance against flooding, against earthquakes in a country like Japan is very important. Limiting choice is also helping people making choices more easily.

Last but not least, I would like to say that we really believe at the OECD that financial education should always be coupled with appropriate consumer protection, financial consumer protection. There is no way you can educate people if the disclosure requirements are not adapted to consumers in the country if the redress mechanisms are not appropriate.

Now a few words about what we are trying to do about this challenge and how we see our work ahead. By the way, this is what we are planning to do, but we are welcoming suggestions from you because we are here to serve you. First, we have developed a lot of policy instruments over the years. Now we have eight policy instruments, not only the High-level Principles on National Strategies, but many others targeting different audiences, but also good practices, looking at insurance and pensions. So we want to consolidate all that to make sure that you have a single instrument that you can use on financial education. It is supposed to be consumer-friendly and this is what we are aiming at this coming year, together with a methodology to implement that, and this is the policy handbook we will deliver to the G20 this year.

Second, we want to have a look at good practices and good practices need to be evaluated. So at the moment we are collecting information on programs that have been evaluated. We are collecting information on the program, on the evaluation methodology, and the results, and we will make that available to all of you on our website. We are also developing a checklist on how to evaluate programs.

Of course, third, we are looking at evidence and we want to build more cross-comparable evidence. This was mentioned by Dean Yoshino. Yes, we need cross-comparable evidence and we are really committed to do that. So we will have a survey on financial literacy and inclusion. In 2015, I am encouraging all the countries in the room to participate. The results will be available next year. Also, we are doing the same thing for youth, through the Programme for International Student Assessment (PISA) financial literacy exercise. We are also developing benchmarks on what a young person, and on what an adult should know or should be able to do in respect of finance and this is what we call core competency for youth and adults.

Then we also think that it is very important to build synergies between policymakers and researchers and for this we created a research committee within our network and we have some eminent representatives from this research committee here today and yesterday. It is very important to do that and one direction we are going is indeed to try and develop indicators not only of financial literacy, capability if you prefer, but also of financial wellbeing. This is something that we are really committed to and will develop. If you are interested in the subject, please come and see us because this really is a field that deserves some smart minds to think about it. So please come and help us doing that.

Then, of course, we are looking at different target audiences. We were doing that in the past and we will continue to do so—women, youth, also small and medium-sized enterprises (SMEs), and, of course, we will also—as mentioned by Mr. Tamaki yesterday during the dinner—look at the implication of the variation in the foreign currency rates, for financial education. Last but not least, we are doing a lot of work now on digital finance and the implication of digital finance for financial education and financial consumer protection, and also how digital tools can be used to develop financial education, for developing financial literacy. Thank you very much.

Dean Naoyuki Yoshino: Thank you. Next, Mr. Miles Larbey.

Miles Larbey, Senior Executive Leader, Financial Literacy, ASIC and member of the OECD/INFE Advisory Board: Thank you. I do not have a lot prepared by way of formal comments. I think we have heard quite a lot about the sort of themes emerging from the symposium and essentially some of the challenges that we are looking at here in terms of longer life expectancy, the issue of trust in the financial system, financial exclusion, low levels of financial literacy in some cases, etc. Some of the responses or solutions that we might look at regarding financial education strategies linked with financial inclusion and consumer protection involve the use of behavioral economics and technology. These obviously can play a significant role and provide an opportunity to develop innovative and appropriate products, perhaps to fill some of the gaps and rebuild some of the trust that people may have lost.

We have talked about the importance of schools, starting young, but there are the challenges that come with that in terms of teacher training and good quality resources and influencing the curriculum of course. To me, these are the main takeaways or themes that have emerged, but I thought it might be interesting to contribute something a bit different, to talk a bit about the Australian experience, the Australian perspective. As we heard yesterday, it is one of the countries that was developing or had developed a second national strategy. So I thought it might be interesting to take a minute or two to talk about how this new strategy, the one that we launched in August last year, differed or what lessons we learned or how it changed from the previous one.

The first national strategy in Australia was launched in 2011 and really, looking back on it now, we all thought it was terrific at the time and it certainly was a lot of work, but it was really a strategy for the Australian Securities and Investments Commission (ASIC) as the financial conduct regulator in Australia and the body responsible for financial literacy at the government level. So it was really a document that set out what we were going to do and how we were going to do it. At that time, we were still making the case for the importance of financial literacy and a lot of it therefore was that sort of narrative, that sort of approach. It did not have any specific measureable targets in it, very deliberately, because we did not know what we were going to be able to achieve and so on.

We did commit to reviewing it in a number of years' time and that is the process that we kicked off to lead to the new one. I think the new strategy that we have—now these things are always evolving and we will always be learning—is a significant step forward from the first one. Firstly, in order to develop that strategy, we conducted probably the largest consultation exercise that ASIC has ever done because whereas most of ASIC's activities affect particular sectors within the financial services industry and maybe consumer and investor representatives, the financial education strategy really involves people from so many different sectors—nongovernment organizations (NGOs), government, for us federal, state, territory, local government as well as industry, the education sector, and the training sector. So it was a very significant consultation exercise that took about a year, with a number of public forums, bilateral meetings, consultation processes, and so on. What we have ended up with is a strategy that is much more—it is truly a national strategy. It is a much more holistic approach. It is high-level in some respects because—recognizing that financial education is a broad church—we want as many organizations as possible that are operating in this area to look at the national strategy and see it as a home for what they are doing in that strategy. So that they, whether it is something that they are doing as a key part of their business or whether it is just tangential to something else they are doing, can see how they are contributing to the national strategy. This should apply whether people are running existing programs or want to develop new programs, whether they are large organizations or small organizations.

I think that has been a galvanizing factor and it has re-energized the stakeholders in terms of their commitment to financial literacy. Because they can sign up and declare, I am supporting the national strategy.

Another thing that is different is there is a much greater commitment to research, measurement, and evaluation in this strategy. We have heard a lot about that over the course of the sessions, but certainly the strategy is not only looking for better ways to measure success here in terms of evaluation of programs and certainly ASIC is seeing the importance of that. I mentioned some new research we have been doing about tracking behaviors and attitudes, but there needs to be a strong push for programs to be evaluated and for those results to be shared.

The strategy has indicators of success in it, which, as I said, the previous one did not. So it sets out five strategic priorities and in relation to each of those priorities, there are a number of key performance indicators, if you like. They are not too prescriptive because we do not know if we will be able to meet them—we do not know how things will go over the next few years, but there is certainly a commitment. We will benchmark ourselves and then measure and report back on that.

The strategy also has a very clear commitment to taking learnings from behavioral economics, to apply them to issues such as use of defaults, product settings, and policy settings. They work in a very complementary way with financial education. We can apply some of the findings of behavioral economics or behavioral insights, to our approach to financial education. So things like single step, single calls to action, or just-in-time delivery of information, or whatever it might be, there is a lot that we can learn and build into our programs and our approach.

The strategy also has a strong commitment to technology. Certainly at ASIC we have made all of our website offerings mobile-friendly, so they can be used on smartphones and tablets and so on.

Finally, to pick up on the point that Ms. Messy has been making, which we certainly agree with strongly too, the strategy clearly sets out this is financial education, this is what we think it can do, and this is what we think it cannot do, or rather, this is how it fits in or needs to fit into the jigsaw of financial inclusion, consumer protection, and fair and efficient markets as well. Putting it in a sort of broader context, we see it very much as strongly supporting ASIC's consumer protection and regulatory work. The two can go hand in hand, so that you are focusing on both the demand side and the supply side in terms of responses.

Dean Naoyuki Yoshino: Thank you very much. Our next speaker is from Viet Nam. Mr. Nguyen is from the central bank of Viet Nam and I hope you can talk about your experience in the Asian region.

Nguyen Vinh Hung, Deputy Director General, International Cooperation Department, State Bank of Vietnam: First, I would like to thank ADBI, OECD, Bank of Japan, and FSA for organizing this symposium. For the last two days, we have heard about financial education practice sin various countries. We will all agree on the importance of financial education. I was very interested in the presentations from Australia and Japan on financial education in their formal education system.

More than any in other country, I think, in Viet Nam we are in need of good information because Viet Nam is quite far behind other countries in terms of financial education. The key messages I can take home from this symposium will be that for financial education, we need joint and comprehensive efforts from various entities to ensure the success of the program. In order to have a good financial education program, we need to get both the demand side and the supply side of financial education involved, as I think the government cannot do the job alone.

We need to get the involvement of training centers, universities, financial institutions, and social entities, to ensure the program will be practical, feasible, and sustainable. In my view, one difficult job is how to measure the financial literacy level in a country, especially in a country like Viet Nam—how to measure the demand for financial education in order to have a good national program for financial education? As I mentioned earlier, in order to implement the financial education program successfully, we need to get the involvement of the various entities or stakeholders.

I think in the case of Viet Nam, we should get the involvement of the private sector to utilize the expertise and experience of the private sector in financial education. We also need the experience, expertise, and resources from international sources and other countries to prepare our national financial education program. All the presentations in this symposium were very informative for me, and for the future work of the State Bank of Vietnam. Definitely first thing next Monday, I will go to the OECD website for your research. Thank you.

Dean Naoyuki Yoshino: Let me put several questions to all of you and then I would like to open the discussion to the floor. First, I think Ms. Messy was talking about coordination between academics, policymakers, and industry. I think that is very important. In Japan, we are doing relatively well compared to other countries. Academic societies are all involved in those issues and we have lots of academic discussions. But if the OECD could distribute the data and survey results to various countries' academics, I think that would enhance their research on financial education. So I hope you can disclose those survey data and so on; it will be very important.

Second, many people would like to know how to measure the enhancement of wellbeing. What kind of data should we look at? The final goal is to enhance the wellbeing of many individuals in each nation. Should we look at the savings rate or consumption? What kind of measures should we look at? The performance of many programs is evaluated based on how many seminars have been conducted, how many people attended, the degree of satisfaction, and so on. The final goal is the wellbeing of many people. So I would like to ask the academics, what kind of measurements should we look at?

Third, behavioral economics is very important. If financial education is well implemented, could we avoid bubbles and financial crises? We have seen in some cases at the start of a crisis many people started investing in the housing market and everybody else followed. Then, could financial education prevent those kinds of crises or bubbles? That would be ideal.

Last, Asia is still very different from the advanced nations in terms of microcredit, microfinance, SMEs, and so on. So financial education programs should be different for two different kinds of groups—for those countries with well-developed financial systems and for those emerging nations where financial activities may be slower to develop. I think lots of different levels of financial education systems may be important. If some of you could answer those questions first, I would like to ask you to do so. Ms. Messy?

Ms. Flore-Anne Messy: Yes, of course, I am happy to start. Yes, on the cooperation between academics, policymakers, and industry, I am very impressed with what is being done in Japan and I think it is excellent practice because researchers seem really to be at the disposal of policymakers and vice versa to make things better. So at the international level we created this research committee precisely to share the surveys and the data that we are producing.

First of all, the PISA data on financial literacy are available online. So you can have access to all the datasets—that is completely public. Concerning the survey of financial literacy and inclusion for adults, the results are also public and of course we will do the survey with the countries that are participating in the exercise in 2015, and of course our goal is to publish the results. We will also make the dataset available to the researchers who are members of our INFE research committee (countries permitting). They have a specific website where they can share data and discuss research.

The objective is not at all to keep all this information within the OECD. We are doing all that work for countries and also to interact with the academic world. So, really, the purpose is to make that public.

The second question on wellbeing and financial wellbeing, I would like to address that in particular. Yes, we are starting to work on indicators of financial wellbeing, which may include a number of variables, to be very honest. The first one, and probably the most obvious one, is whether people are satisfied with their financial situation. This is a question that is very subjective, but wellbeing is subjective as well, so this is one of the questions that we introduced in our new questionnaire that we will use in 2015.

In addition to that, we also know that financial wellbeing is very much correlated with whether people are in control of their finances, whether they have a budget, whether they are able to plan ahead. In addition to that, a lot of research is using concepts that are very close to what financial literacy is about—being in control of your budget, being able to plan ahead. So these are behaviors that are already captured by financial literacy indicators.

It is interesting to see that financial wellbeing is not only defined as something subjective and unique to particular individuals, but also with respect to time. So if people have the expectation that their financial situation will get better in future, this is very important for their present financial wellbeing. This is one of the questions that you may want to consider as well.

You need to compare over time, but people also tend to compare with others—do they believe that their financial literacy situation is favorable compared with others? This is another thing to consider and probably valuable to consider. I am being very modest here because I am sure I can learn from you and all the researchers in the room, and I am sure you have other ideas. But this is the direction of our thinking and of course if you have other ideas, they are most welcome because this is a subject that we want to discuss, to open up, and work more on in the future.

Regarding the question whether financial education can prevent future financial crises, well, the simple answer would be no. No, I think again we need to be low-key and modest here. Financial education can probably prevent the very negative and long-lasting consequences of financial crises. If people understand what is happening, maybe their behavior will be more rational. Rationality is very subjective. Sometimes economists believe that people are not behaving in a rational way, but actually they are very rational considering their situation. So yes, what we believe is probably that the negative consequences can be less important.

After the crisis we have seen many people really affected because, for example, they had bought financial products or investment products that they thought had no risks attached to them when in fact these products were extremely risky in the first place. Maybe financial education can help, but again, if disclosure requirements about these products were not appropriate and there was no way a normal consumer could understand that there were actually risks associated with the product, I am not sure this would help either. So we really think financial education should work in conjunction with appropriate regulation, supervision, and consumer protection to be effective.

Regarding your last question about Asia, saying Asia is so different. Do we need a different type of financial education? Do we need a different type of financial education for developed and developing countries? I think the national strategy framework is there to be adapted to the country's circumstances, really. Some of the countries will have as a priority financial inclusion and access, so they will need to deal with the supply side and make sure that suitable products are accessible to a larger portion of the population. They will still try to provide the basic financial literacy for people to actually use the products.

In other countries, probably you are dealing with aging, a situation where the population is aging and you have pension reform and this is sophisticated kind of knowledge that people will want or need. But I am not sure that we need different types of financial education. I think everybody should have the basics—the planning ahead, being in control of your finance, having some reasonable knowledge of key financial concepts is probably common across countries. Then what can be specific is, indeed, some target audiences that would benefit particularly from financial education. But I have to say that, for example, microentrepreneurs and SMEs, are an area of opportunity in Asia, but also in Africa, Latin America, Europe increasingly, and even the United States. I mean these kinds of target audiences also exist elsewhere and also have a need for financial literacy.

So I would say you need the diagnosis, the evidence, and then probably you want to target some of your financial education to particular groups, but the whole population will need the very basic concepts and skills to adapt to changes.

***Dean Naoyuki Yoshino*:** Thank you. Mr. Larbey, any comments?

***Mr. Miles Larbey*:** Yes, thanks. Well, I agree with a lot of what Ms. Messy was saying. I think in terms of measuring wellbeing, that is a difficult thing because wellbeing is obviously a subjective notion in many respects to an individual, a family, or a community. Certainly, we know through our financial education efforts that part of our objective, primary objective is to improve people's sense of wellbeing.

So in Australia what we have done is, we asked ourselves how are we going to measure changes or progress or how do we know if we are making any difference to people's sense of wellbeing? Because, as I said, it is a subjective idea, but also a matter of trying to isolate people's behaviors or attitudes that might suggest one person has a greater sense of financial wellbeing than another. That invariably involves lots of other issues, such as how much income do they have or what other influences or contexts are they operating in, what is the external environment, what is their personal history, and so on and so forth.

We have—and this is through our new tracking research—tried to work within the overall framework of what a financially literate person might look like, or what behaviors they might exhibit. This means trying to isolate some behaviors or attitudes that, without making any value judgments, might be considered to be characteristic of someone who is more likely to be more financially literate and have a greater sense of financial wellbeing than not. That is a huge generalization but there we are.

It does come down to things like a sense of control, having a financial plan, a feeling of being stressed or not being stressed, confident in managing your money or control of your money. It is hard to say that having a day-to-day budget in place could really be a bad thing for anybody, regardless of their income, age, or personal circumstances. So we are trying, it is a difficult thing to do, but I think it is important nonetheless that we do that.

Interestingly, what we found from our first wave of tracking research is that in many respects, when it comes to financial attitudes, there is no huge difference between people with lower incomes versus people with higher incomes in terms of the levels of satisfaction, but certainly there are varying attitudes. For example, a feeling that nothing I can do will make a difference is one area where people with lower incomes do seem to have different results from people on higher incomes, but more research needs to be done.

In terms of behavioral economics—sorry, financial education preventing financial crisis—yes, I think it is a part of the solution, but it will never be the solution. One of the reasons why the Investor Education Centre in Hong Kong, China that I set up was established was precisely because of the Lehman minibonds mis-selling scandal that hit Hong Kong, China and other parts of Asia. So a lot of our investor education was focused on risk and return, and understanding products and diversification, and so on.

In Australia we had a series of collapses. People had invested in unlisted and unrated debenture schemes, property schemes, and these schemes collapsed and people lost money and we asked people, some of the victims, did they understand diversification and so on? They absolutely said, yes, they had and they thought their portfolios were diversified because they had invested in two property schemes with the same fund manager, so that was a diversified portfolio. So it is financial education, understanding risks, investor education—that is obviously an important part of how people will be prepared for or respond to future financial crises.

In terms of differences between Asia and other regions or jurisdictions, I agree with Ms. Messy. As someone who has worked in Hong Kong, China and in Australia in relation to financial education, a lot of the overarching objectives were the same. Absolutely, in terms of, say, investor education or financial planning or money management. It might be that some of the characteristics of the population or some of the specific issues were different. Certainly in Hong Kong, China, people tend to have a very high savings rate, whereas in Australia people are more likely to be repaying debt. So you might be approaching certain economies differently. And in Hong Kong, China, people are much more direct participants in the market, whereas in Australia that tends to be more through retirement savings or managed funds or something.

There are different population characteristics and different issues, but at a broad level, I think, the objectives and many of the approaches actually are very similar.

Dean Naoyuki Yoshino: Thank you very much.

Closing Remarks

Rintaro Tamaki, OECD Deputy Secretary-General: Distinguished guests, experts, ladies and gentlemen, good afternoon. I wish to start by conveying again my sincere gratitude to our co-host, ADBI, and co-organizers, the FSA and Bank of Japan. I would also like to thank the Japanese—my—government for its continued support of OECD activities on financial education in Asia and for its particular contribution to this event.

Turning to our subject matter, let me once again stress how the global financial and economic context as well as demographic and social trends represent at the same time a challenge and an important impetus. The fallout that we have seen borne by individuals makes financial literacy skills essential in the 21st century. These are especially important to support effective, forward-looking life planning for youths and adults. Your attendance at this international gathering has further confirmed the relevance of financial education and its contribution globally and for Asia.

And I would like to thank you all, and especially speakers, moderators, and commentators, for sharing your relevant expertise and know-how. Your contributions have elevated the debate and helped us to identify new areas for research, analysis, and progress.

I will not attempt to summarize all of our very rich discussions, especially as the previous wrap-up session provided us with the key highlights from the different panels. However, I would briefly like to point to a few selected take-aways from this event:

- First, while acknowledging the importance of financial education, we all also recognize that it has its limitations. To effectively support individuals' financial planning, financial education initiatives need to happen in an adequate and enabling environment. This comprises first financial access for all, appropriate financial consumer protection, and sound regulation and supervision. This enabling framework also involves the establishment of a national strategy for financial education. Such a strategy should ensure a multi-stakeholder, coordinated action, the setting of commonly agreed goals, as well as inclusive and effective practices. It should also support the development of financial literacy skills early in life.

- Second, when dealing with pension management, financial education should be tailored to the existing pension system. It should also take account of the levels of individuals' autonomy and responsibility in the particular system as well as their levels of financial literacy and awareness. Financial education should be made instrumental in pension reform and in creating greater awareness of the importance of starting to save early and appropriately.

- Third, motivation, culture, learning preferences, and the interest of particular groups such as women or young people should be carefully assessed and the importance of timing should not be overlooked. These parameters will be essential when designing financial education initiatives and providing financial information to these groups in an effective way.

- Fourth, I would like to insist again on the importance of developing policies and practices based on evidence. Luckily, policymakers now have at their disposal international and OECD tools recognized by G20 leaders, that they can use to tailor more suitable initiatives. I would thus like to encourage all countries to participate in the planned second INFE adult survey on financial literacy and inclusion in 2015 and the future PISA financial literacy exercise in 2018. Evidence also has to come from appropriate and systematic monitoring and evaluation of financial education initiatives. Here again,

I would like to invite you all to support the OECD/INFE in developing a global database of evaluated financial education programs.

- Last, I would like to flag that the OECD and its network will continue to be committed to the development of evidence and policy tools, and is currently developing an international benchmark on financial literacy core competencies for young people to be delivered to G20 leaders this year. This should ensure that a consistent approach is adopted to identify financial education goals and monitor progress.

Your contribution to all of these endeavors is essential and I would like to thank you for your active contribution to our common goal. I wish you all an enjoyable stay in Tokyo, and a safe and pleasant trip back home.

I also hope to see you in Paris in May at our next INFE meeting and Global Policy Research Symposium which will focus on financial literacy and SMEs—a very topical subject for this year's G20 Turkish Presidency. In the meantime, I invite you to join me for lunch, kindly hosted by the Bank of Japan.

Thank you.

References[*]

Asian Development Bank (ADB). 2008. *Protection Index for Committed Poverty Reduction, Volume II (Asia)*. Manila: ADB.

Agnew, J., L. Szykman, S. Utkus, and J. Young. 2012. Trust, Plan Knowledge and 401(k) Savings Behavior. *Journal of Pension Economics and Finance* 11(1): 1–20.

Agnew, J., and J. Hurwitz. 2013. Financial Education and Choice in State Public Pension Systems. NBER Working Paper 18907. Cambridge, MA: National Bureau of Economic Research. http://www.nber.org/papers/w18907.

Atkinson, A., and F. Messy. 2012. Measuring Financial Literacy: Results of the OECD/International Network on Financial Education (INFE) Pilot Study. OECD Working Papers on Finance, Insurance and Private Pensions No. 15. Paris: OECD. http://dx.doi.org/10.1787/5k9csfs90fr4-en.

Brown, J., A. Farrell, and S. Weisbenner. 2011. The Downside of Defaults. NBER Retirement Research Center Paper NB11-01. Cambridge, MA: National Bureau of Economic Research. http://www.nber.org/aging/rrc/papers/orrc11-01.

Brown, J., and S. Weisbenner. 2014. Why Do Individuals Choose Defined Contribution Plans? Evidence from Participants in a Large Public Plan. *Journal of Public Economics* 116: 35–46.

Central Council for Financial Services Information (CCFSI). 2002. *Guidelines for the Promotion of Consumer Education on Finance*. Tokyo: Central Council for Financial Services Information.

———. 2012. *Japan Financial Literacy Survey*. Tokyo: Central Council for Financial Services Information.

---

[*] The Asian Development Bank refers to China by the name People's Republic of China.

Choi, J., D. Laibson, B. Madrian, and A. Metrick. 2002. Defined Contribution Pensions: Plan Rules, Participant Decisions and the Path of Least Resistance. In *Tax Policy and the Economy*, edited by J.M. Poterba. Cambridge, MA: MIT Press. pp. 67–113.

Choi, J., D. Laibson, B. Madrian, and A. Metrick. 2006. Saving for Retirement on the Path of Least Resistance. In *Behavioral Public Finance: Toward a New Agenda*, edited by E. McCaffrey and J. Slemrod. New York: Russell Sage Foundation.

Clark, R., A. Lusardi, and O. Mitchell. 2014. Financial Knowledge and 401(k) Investment Performance. Pension Research Council Working Paper WP2014-03.

FINRA Investor Education Foundation. 2013. *Financial Capability in the US: Report of Findings of the 2012 National Financial Capability Survey*. Washington, DC: FINRA Investor Education Foundation.

García, N., A. Grifoni, J. López, and D. Mejía. 2013. Financial Education in Latin America and the Caribbean: Rationale, Overview and Way Forward. OECD Working Papers on Finance, Insurance and Private Pensions No. 33. Paris: OECD. http://dx.doi.org/10.1787/5k41zq7hp6d0-en.

Japan Management and Coordination Agency Statistics Bureau. 2013. Population Estimate. Tokyo: Management and Coordination Agency.

MasterCard. 2013. China Overtakes Hong Kong with the Most Proficient Investors in Asia/Pacific: MasterCard Index of Financial Literacy. 3 July. http://www.masterintelligence.com/content/intelligence/en/research/press-release/2013/china-overtakes-hongkong-with-the-most-proficient-investors-in-asia-pacific-mastercard-index-of-financial-literacy.html.

National Agency for Financial Studies (NAFI). 2013. *Encyclopedia on the Financial Behavior of Russians*. Moscow: NAFI.

National Social Welfare and Population Research Institute. 2012. Japan's Future Population Estimate. Tokyo: National Social Welfare and Population Research Institute.

Organisation for Economic Co-operation and Development (OECD).2014. *PISA 2012 Results: Students and Money: Financial Literacy Skills for the 21st Century (Volume VI)*. Paris: OECD. http://dx.doi.org/10.1787/9789264208094-en.

Plan Sponsor Council of America (PSCA). 2014. *57th Annual Survey of Profit Sharing and 401(k) Plans*. Chicago, IL: Plan Sponsor Council of America. http://www.psca.org/57thAS_Report.

Study Group on the Promotion of Financial and Economic Education. 2014. *Comprehensive Survey of Financial and Economic Education in Japan's Junior High and High Schools*. Tokyo: Japan Securities Dealers Association.

Tergesen, A. 2011. 401(k) Law Suppresses Saving for Retirement. *Wall Street Journal*. 7 July. http://www.wsj.com/articles/SB1000142405270 2303365804576430153643522780.

Xu, L., and B. Zia. 2012. Financial Literacy around the World: An Overview of the Evidence with Practical Suggestions for the Way Forward. World Bank Policy Research Working Paper No. 6107. Washington, DC: World Bank.

Yoshino, N., P. Morgan, and G. Wignaraja. 2015. Financial Education in Asia: Assessment and Recommendations. ADBI Working Paper 534. Tokyo: Asian Development Bank Institute. http://www.adb.org/publications/financial-education-asia-assessment-and-recommendations.

Printed in the United States
By Bookmasters